Issei Suda

Introduction by Simon Baker

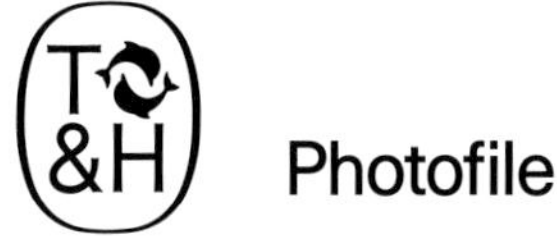

Photofile

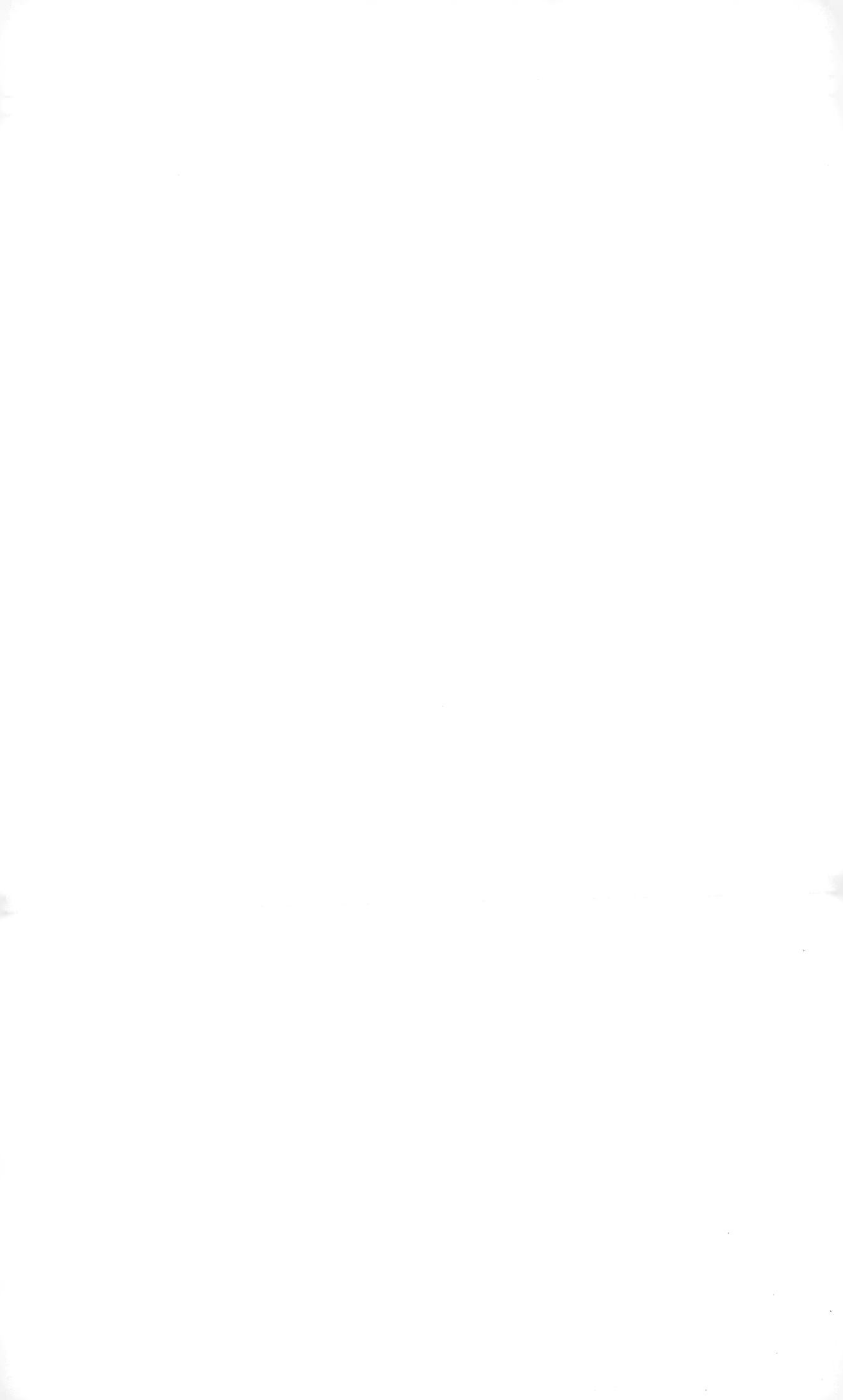

'Myself and my times'[1]

Issei Suda was born in Tokyo in 1940, in the neighbourhood of
Kanda, now famous for the quantity and quality of its bookshops,
a place of pilgrimage for photobook collectors. Although technically
speaking, he began working professionally as a stage photographer
in 1967, documenting Shuji Terayama's avant-garde Tenjo Sajiki group,
Suda's career as a photographer started in earnest in 1971 with the
Fūshi Kaden series, and by 1976 he was recognized as a 'newcomer' of
great promise. And this achievement took place among arguably the
greatest generation of photographers to have emerged simultaneously
in one time and place anywhere in the world. This bold claim was
underlined by the landmark 1974 exhibition at MoMA in New
York, *New Japanese Photography*, in which the new masters of the
new styles like Eikoh Hosoe, Kikuji Kawada, Daido Moriyama and
Shomei Tomatsu, rubbed shoulders with their more conventional
contemporaries, Ken Domon and Yasuhiro Ishimoto: all, however,
being revealed together for the first time to an international audience.

Japan in the early 1970s meant many things for photography,
but most of all, perhaps, it meant a radical reconsideration of the
relationship between subjective and objective conceptions of the
photographic image: the rupture (and being Japan, a polite one),
between the different but complementary *tendances* present in the
New York show, and much that had come before them. Identified as
'pivotal' in the press release for the MoMA show, Shomei Tomatsu
exemplifies within his own development precisely this shift
from humanist documentary to radical subjectivity. The idea

of photography moving beyond its responsible and engaged documentary 'job' in the modern era, however, is a familiar one: familiar in Japan and Europe as far back as the 1920s, with the formal acrobatics of both the New Objectivity and Surrealism. But in late sixties Japan, any such formalism gave way not only to new subject choices and perspectives, but also to a kind of avant-garde grunge aesthetic, 'blurry, grainy and out of focus', as it was described at the time. Moriyama, (Takuma) Nakahira, and their contemporaries, now often associated together with the magazine *Provoke*, sought an immersive encounter with the black-and-white image that often seemed to bleed its (usually) urban subjects right across the page.

Issei Suda, however, despite arriving on the same scene at the same time, had both things in common, and points of difference, with his more established and better-known peers. Like Hosoe and Moriyama, for example, both of whom had photographed and published photobooks about actors and dancers, Suda was deeply interested in avant-garde performance art, choreography and physical theatre. In fact, he took this interest further than many of his contemporaries, theorizing and completely rethinking his photographic practice as a result. Suda was also a committed street photographer, but never transformed the city into wild abstractions, and although he was heavily influenced by historical texts, literature, and cultural theory, he let his images speak for themselves. But most importantly perhaps, although Suda was a visual student of his immediate surroundings, he refused definitively to engage in any kind of social or political posturing or rhetoric as a result. His account of Japan is, rather, one inspired by discovering and capturing what he called 'small surprises … usually dismissed in our world'.[2] And moreover, taking what he admitted as his own 'indifference'[3] to the point of opacity: 'It might be true that my works have a typical Japanese quality,' he said, before going on to admit: 'Even seen through the eyes of the Japanese public, my work can be difficult to understand.'[4]

If we should want to 'understand' Suda as a photographer, the question poses itself, how might we go about it? There are, evidently, specific subjects and series into which his practice can

be divided, although date order is unhelpful for several reasons.
A basic chronology would not necessarily even set out from the
Early Works, made between 1970 and 1975, but would rather begin with
the first published series for which Suda received critical attention:
Fūshi Kaden, begun in 1971 but not serialized in the magazine *Camera
Mainichi* until 1975, before being exhibited in Tokyo in 1977, and only
finally being published, as Suda's first book, in 1978. And many of
Suda's key series are also, like *Fūshi Kaden*, the work of many years
that overlap with other works including, for example, *Anonymous
Man and Woman* (1976–78) and *Childhood Days* (1973–82). Or, for an
even more complicated case, Suda's first significant subject/series,
Osorezan e, which stretches across repeated visits to a remote site of
pilgrimage over almost twenty years, between 1962 and 1980. For the
contemporary viewer, however, recent publications, notably those
completed in the last years of Suda's life with Akio Nagasawa, have
rebalanced Suda's work to take full account of the exquisite quality
of his 70s *Early Works* and so it is probably, now at least, the best
place to start.

*'The way in which [the ragpicker] collects the kind of common things that can
be seen lying around everywhere is exactly the same as way as I carry out my
photography. However, for the person that does the collecting, these things are
definitely not rubbish, rather they provide the excitement of a treasure hunt
and offer an inexhaustible source of discovery.'*[5]

Writing a short introduction to the series *Monogusa Shui*, Suda
makes a characteristic, brutally blunt analogy between his own
practice as a photographer and that of what we used to call in
England a 'rag-and-bone' man: an itinerant ragpicker with a horse
and cart. If he had been less humble, and more susceptible to
anachronistic comparisons, however, Suda may well have made a
further link (or leap) with the nominative logic of the surrealist
'found object'. For the search for the marvellous in surrealism, which
also sometimes involved flea markets, is precisely that outlined by
Suda, both verbally and visually, as a kind of magical eruption of,
and from, the everyday. This, perhaps, is why Suda usually rejected

the more extreme avant-garde abstractions of many of his peers, admitting daytime flash and high contrast, but remaining focused with obsessive clarity. What seems to drive Suda, and what also distinguishes his work from that of so many photographers from the same time is precisely his faith in magic: in the ability of the camera to seize and fix a fragment of the world that briefly and perfectly transcends itself.

A fellow artist, Taeko Tomioka, writing in 1977, described Suda's *Fūshi Kaden* as 'depictions of the dark and extraordinary that humans are hiding inside', thereby exposing 'the shady side of daily life'. But the associated and fugitive 'borderline between the ordinary and the extraordinary'[6] that Suda himself describes in relation to his own work is not always one defined exclusively by darkness, as the photographs now collected together as *Early Works* reveal. There are moments of intense urban poetry as figures emerge and recede simultaneously from the shadows that surround them, but there are also moments of sun-kissed play and labour, even if all of them fall squarely onto Suda's 'borderline'. There is also a strange, willful inconsistency in Suda's early work between furtively stolen scenes, and staged, posed compositions: as though the little boy's haircut would really be aligned with a fence; or the decontextualized mystery of one room from a tatami apartment dragged outside and solarized. But overall we are left with the impression of a kind of omnivorous fascination with the everyday world, its materials and its inhabitants, with the ragpicker's relentless search for overlooked and short-lived treasures, from melting ice-blocks to floating basketballs.

Inspired by a fifteenth-century treatise on Noh theatre, *Fūshi Kaden* means, literally, 'transmission of the flower of acting style'. Although it now stands for Suda's 'mature' style, it in fact stands as perhaps the finest edit of his work to date, once again eschewing consistency in terms of content, but instead settling on a dramatic uniformity in terms of technical approach. Diverse and contradictory to the point of meaninglessness, Suda takes in the theatre of daily life in which theatrical performance is only one of a number of ways to encounter the marvellous. And the 'darkness' identified by Tomioka is finely balanced everywhere by the smiling innocence of children of all ages playing themselves. What we find in Suda's 'indifference' to his subjects is a kind of total openness to his surroundings that ranges from curiosity to absentminded amusement.

The overlapping series that encompasses and outstrips *Fūshi Kaden*, having been started or completed during the same time, *Childhood Days* (1973–82), is more uniform in its approach but replete with the same playful mystery. Those that immediately follow *Fūshi Kaden*, *Anonymous Man and Woman* (1976–78) and *My Tokyo 100* (1979), seem also to have been woven from the same deep, soft cloth. Even in what seems to be conventional street photography, we have the impression of people playing their own part in a photographic drama of which Suda is the director. According to the critic Frits Gierstberg,[7] Suda said of *Anonymous Man and Woman*, that 'of all the people you will meet in your life, only a few of them will make it into the history books' and that everyone else is 'supporting actors'.[8] Anonymity, of course, comes with its own pleasures, and Suda's cast, for the most part at least, is a happy one.

It is very difficult, even in hindsight, to isolate what it is exactly that separates Issei Suda from his peers from whom he seems always somehow distinctly 'apart': a brilliant artist of a golden generation who showed little interest in it. There is, perhaps, his incredible attention to detail on many levels: from his ability to see the truly extraordinary in everyday moments through the lens; to his printing technique, using a special ferrotype plate to glaze his prints. And there is also his modesty in allowing publishers, designers and curators the freedom to work with his images, ceding control and allowing them (and therefore his own work) to surprise him. But there is also his noticeable apartness from the flows of style and fashion that he maintained for himself, despite thinking deeply about photography as a practice. Suda was a teacher, but he claimed not to have spoken much to his students, nor given any lectures, instead wanting to learn from *them*. But none of this is to suggest in any way that the self-proclaimed 'indifferent' Suda did not have both great wisdom to share and his own unique mode of observation: 'In the end', he has said, and in the end he is right, 'both the watcher and the watched are reduced to oneself, [and] in addition, I think that the work is created through the unconscious workings of the world in which we live.'[9]

Simon Baker
Director, MEP, Paris

Notes

1   Issei Suda, *My Japan*, Amsterdam: Fw:Books, 2021, p. 138.

2   Issei Suda, *My Japan*, p. 135.

3   Issei Suda, *My Japan*, p. 134.

4   Issei Suda, *My Japan*, p. 135.

5   Issei Suda, *Nagi no hira: Fragments of Calm*, Tokyo: Tosei-sha, 2013, p. 52.

6   Cited in Issei Suda, *Fūshi Kaden* (1978), Tokyo: Akio Nagasawa Publishing, 2023, p. 145.

7   Frits Gierstberg, curator of the exhibition *Issei Suda: My Japan*, Antwerp: FOMU, 2021.

8   Issei Suda, *My Japan*, p. 132.

9   Issei Suda, *Nagi no hira: Fragments of Calm*, p. 156.

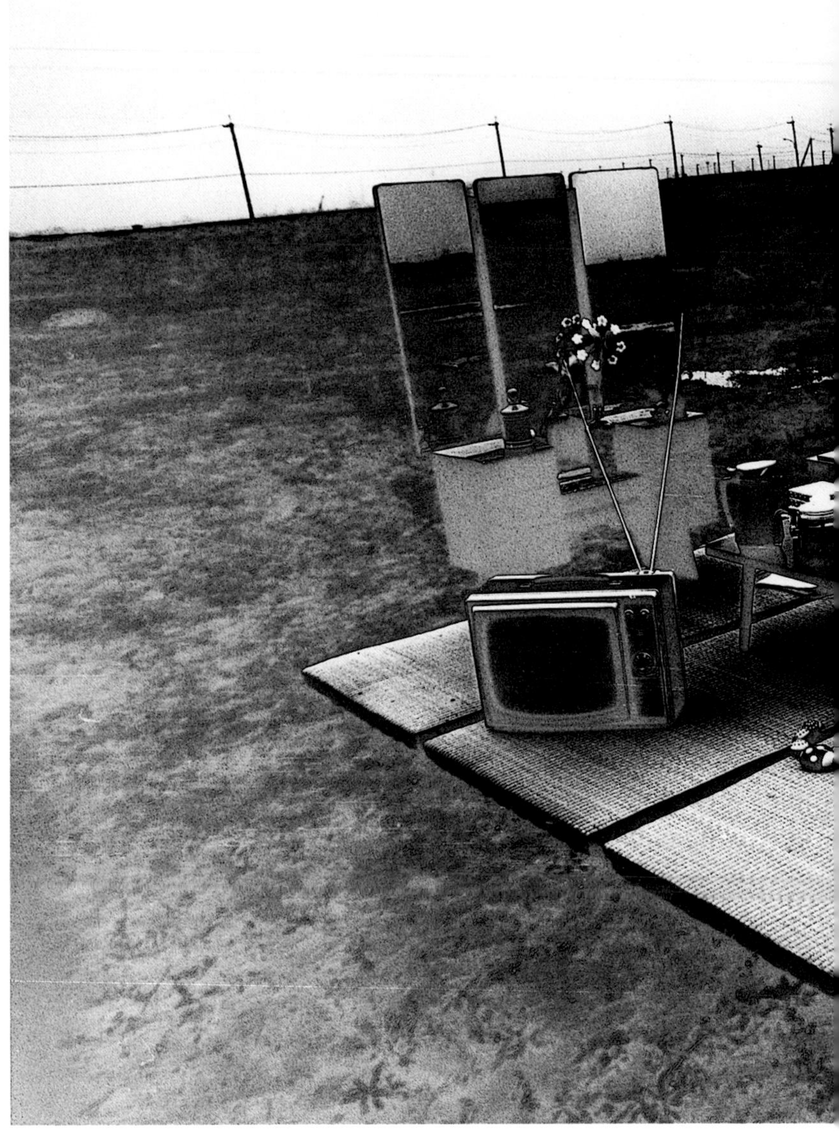

1. *His & Hers*, 1970.

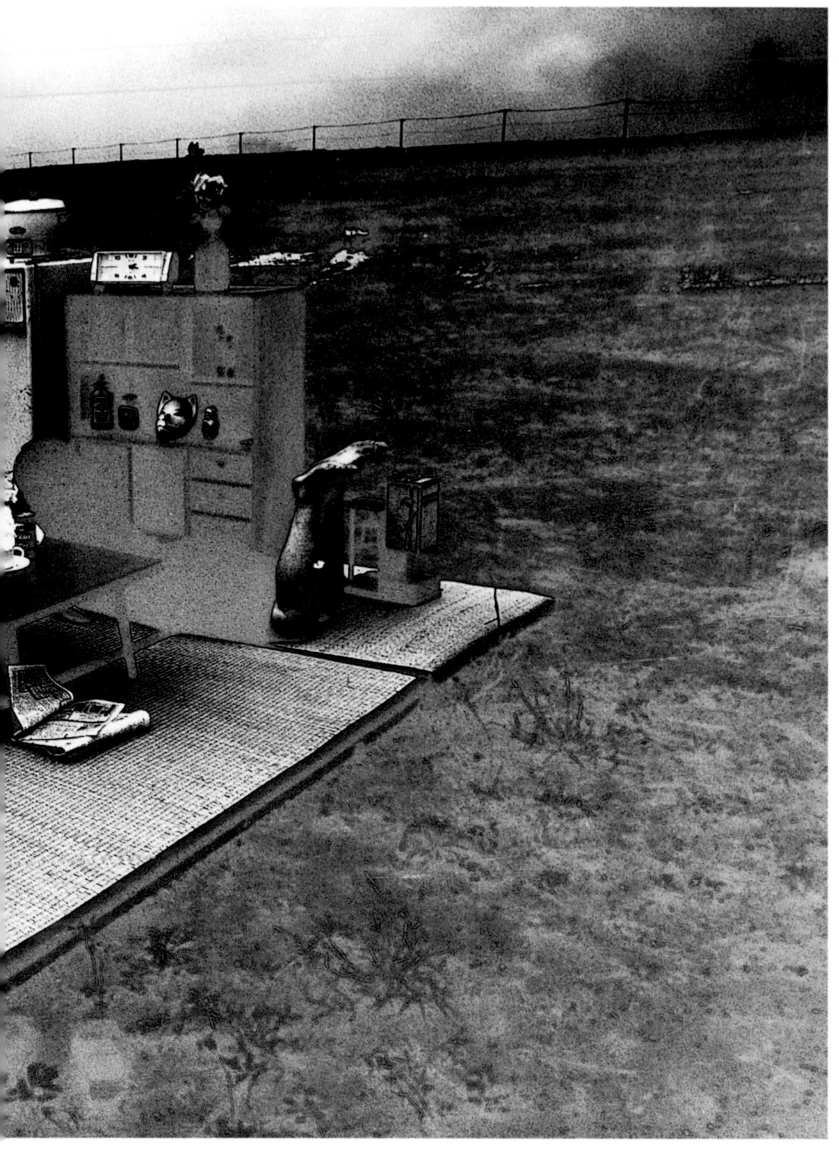

2. *Downtown*, 1968.

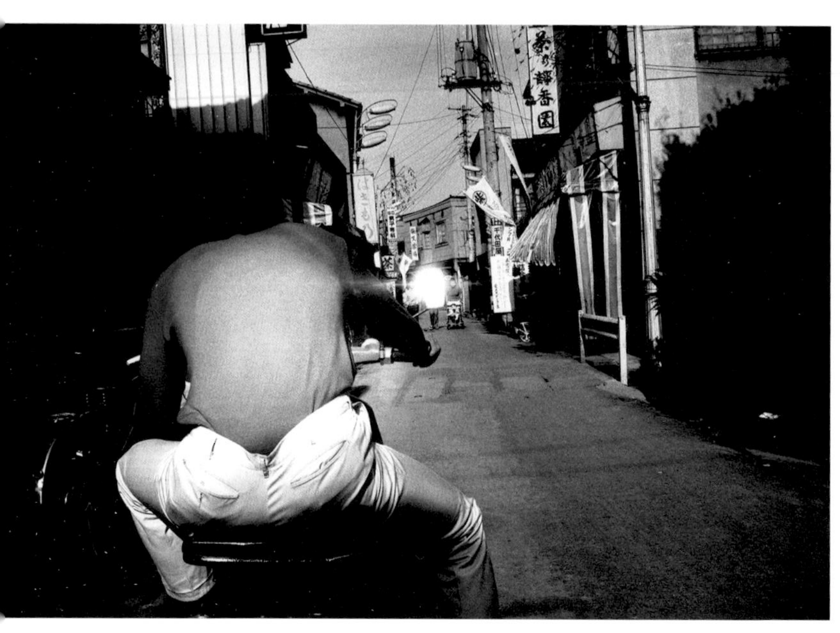

3. *25 Tomiyama-Cho*, 1971.

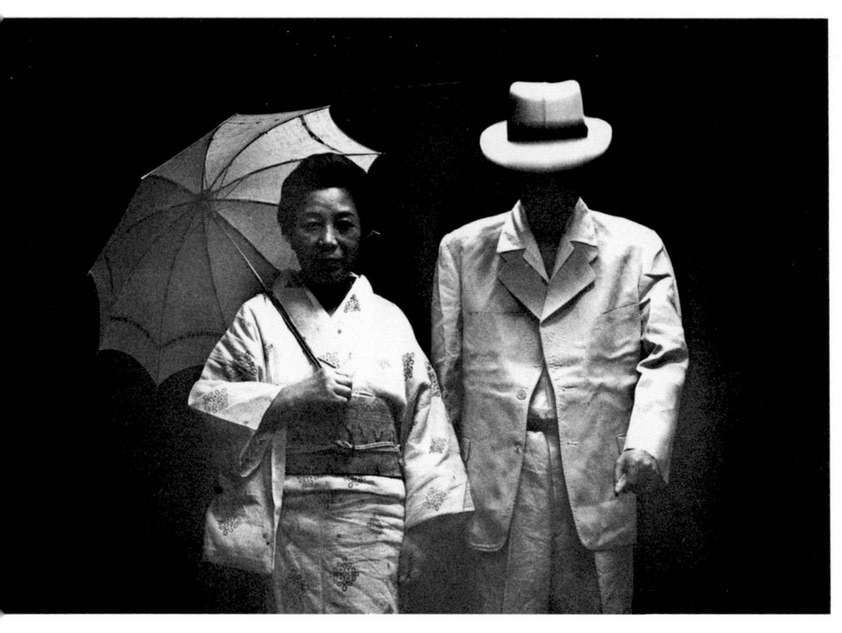

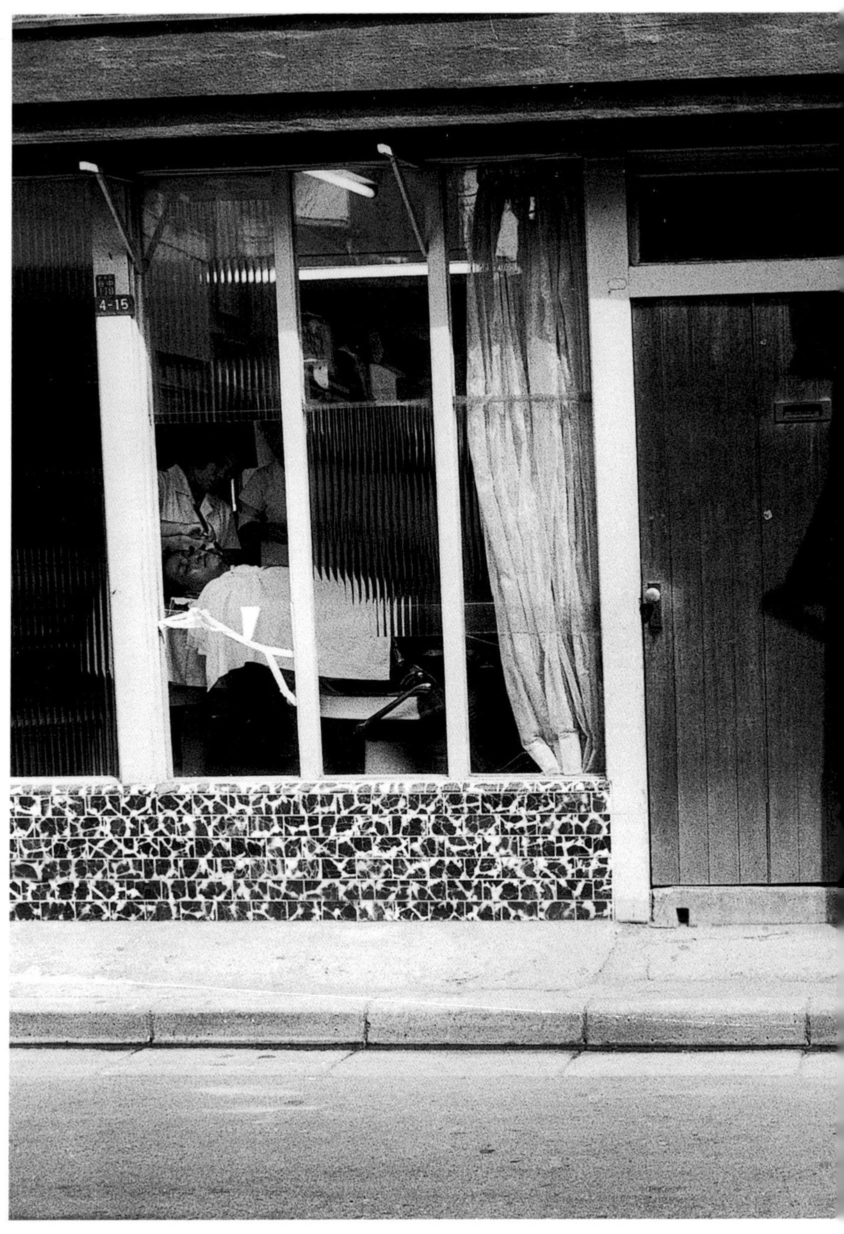

4. *Holiday*, ca. 1970.

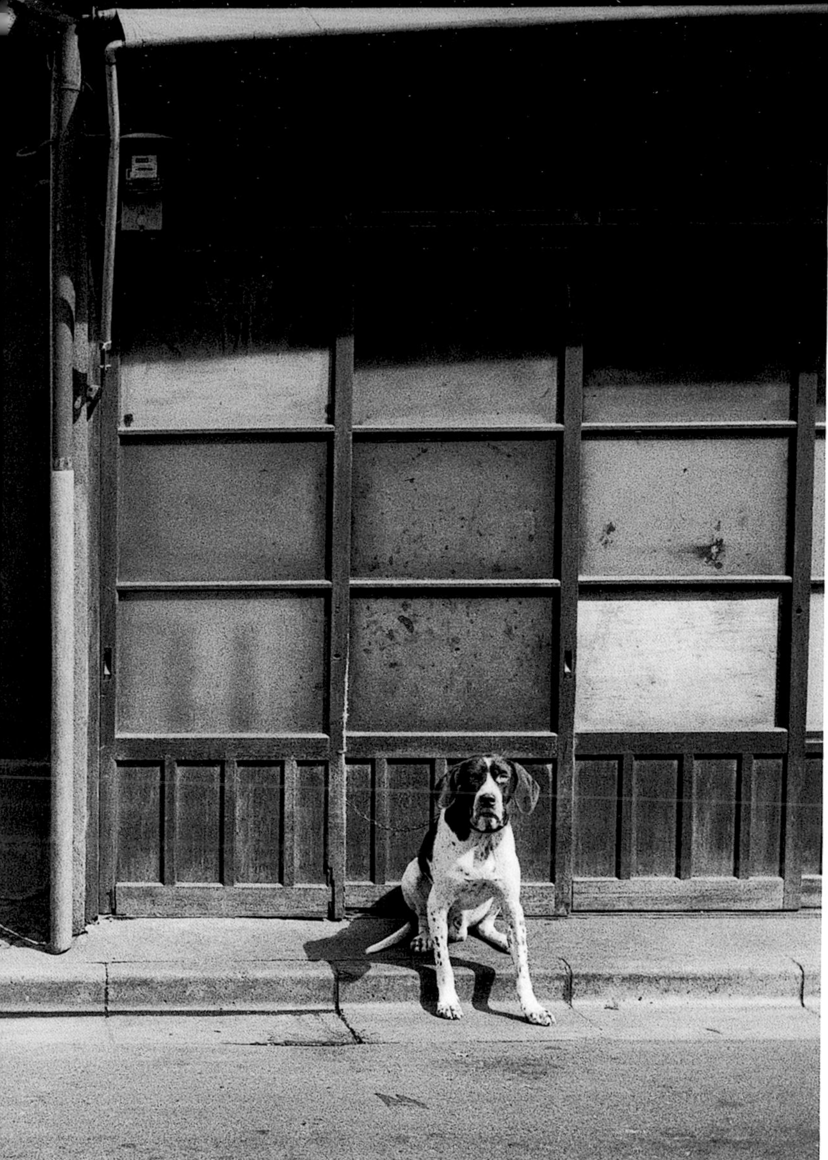

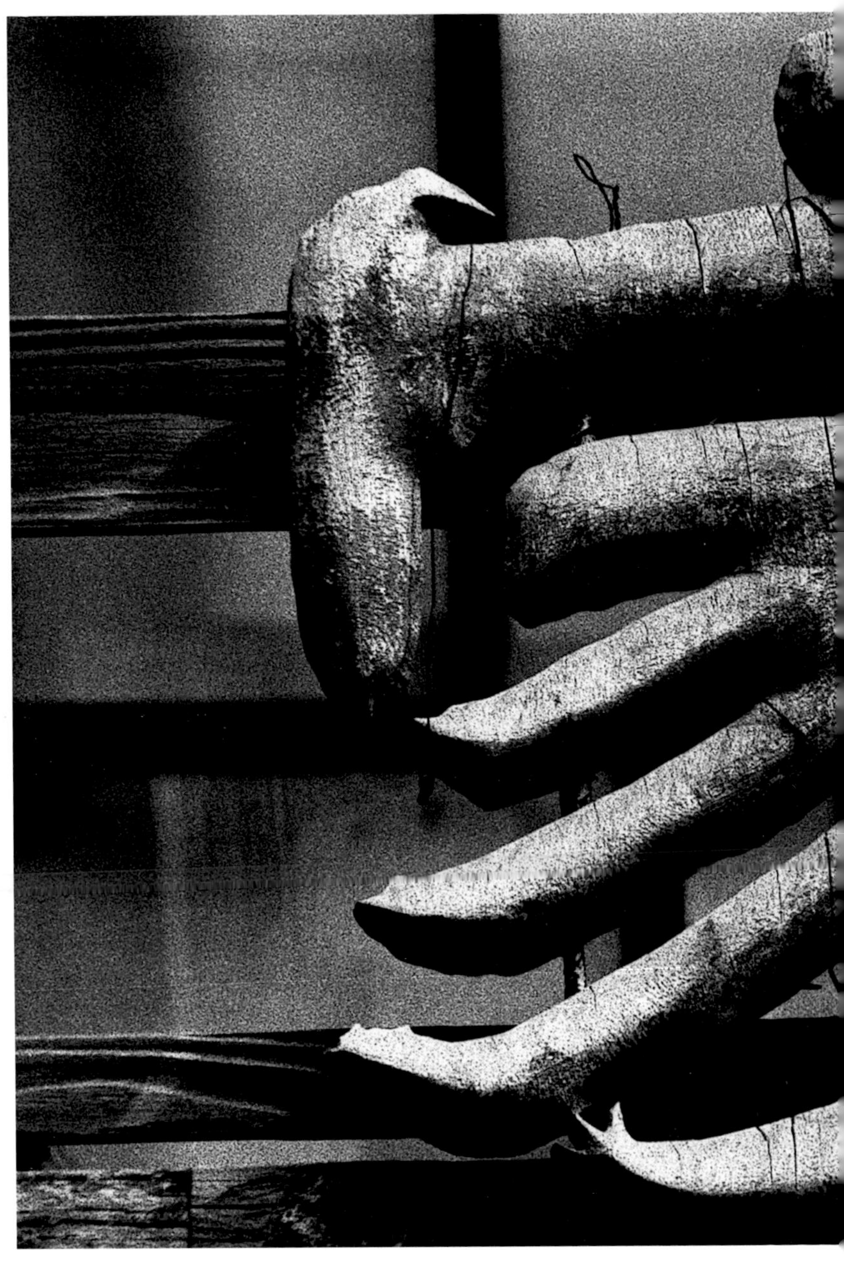

5. *Memory*, 1974.

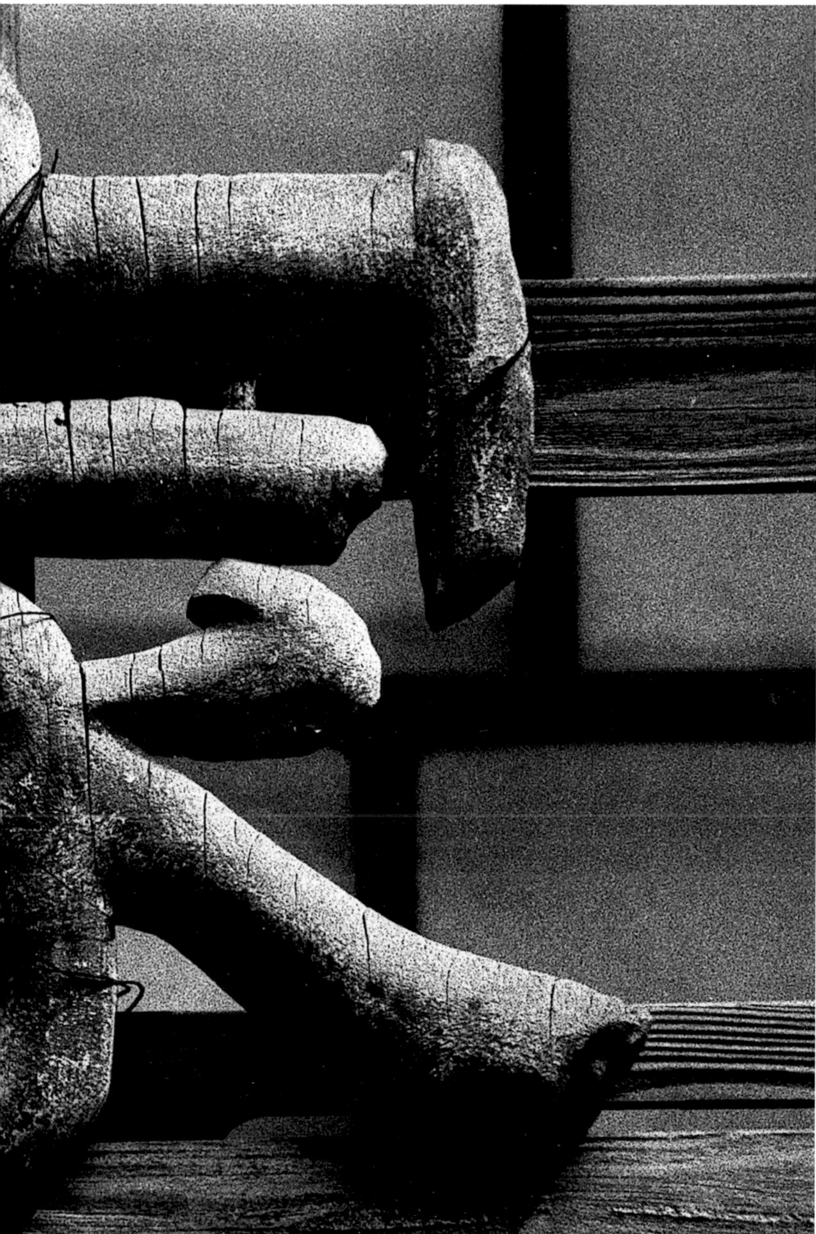

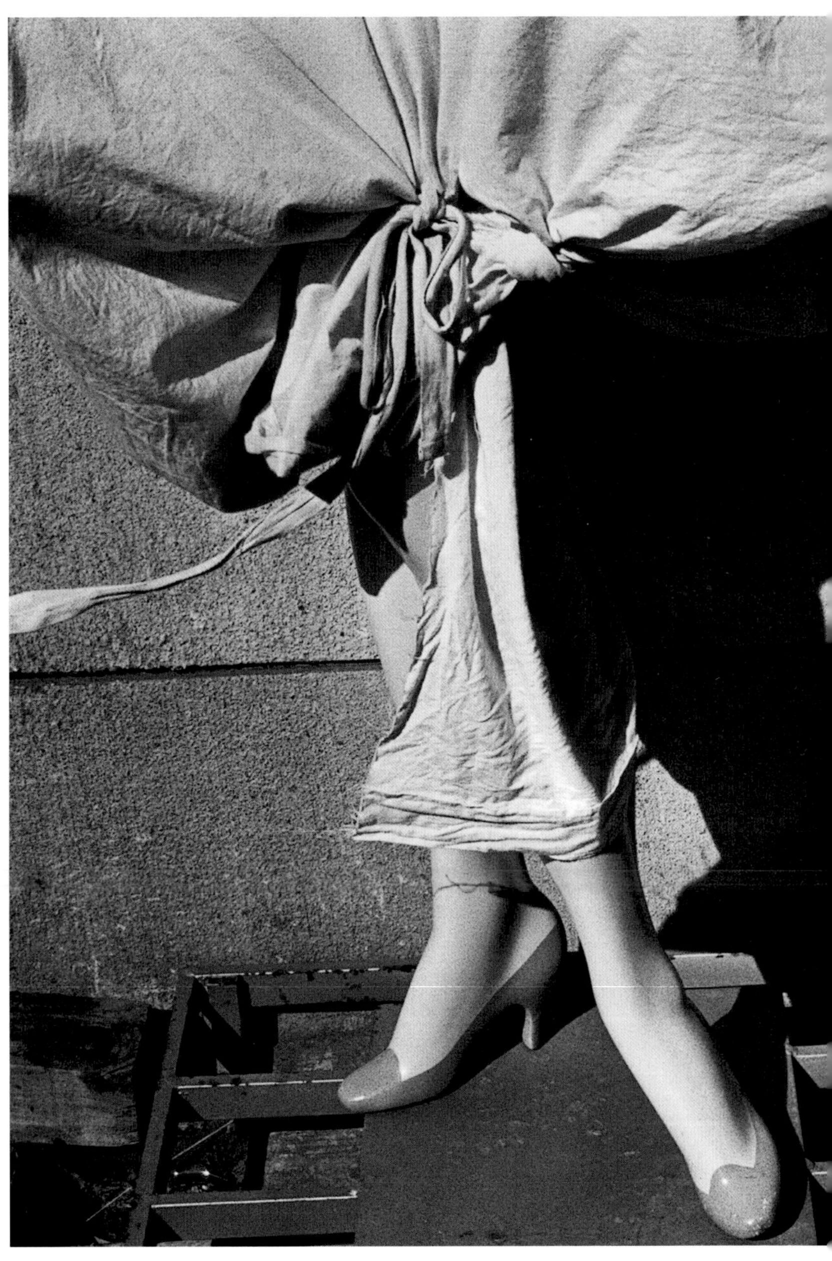

6. *Autumn Candles*, 1973.

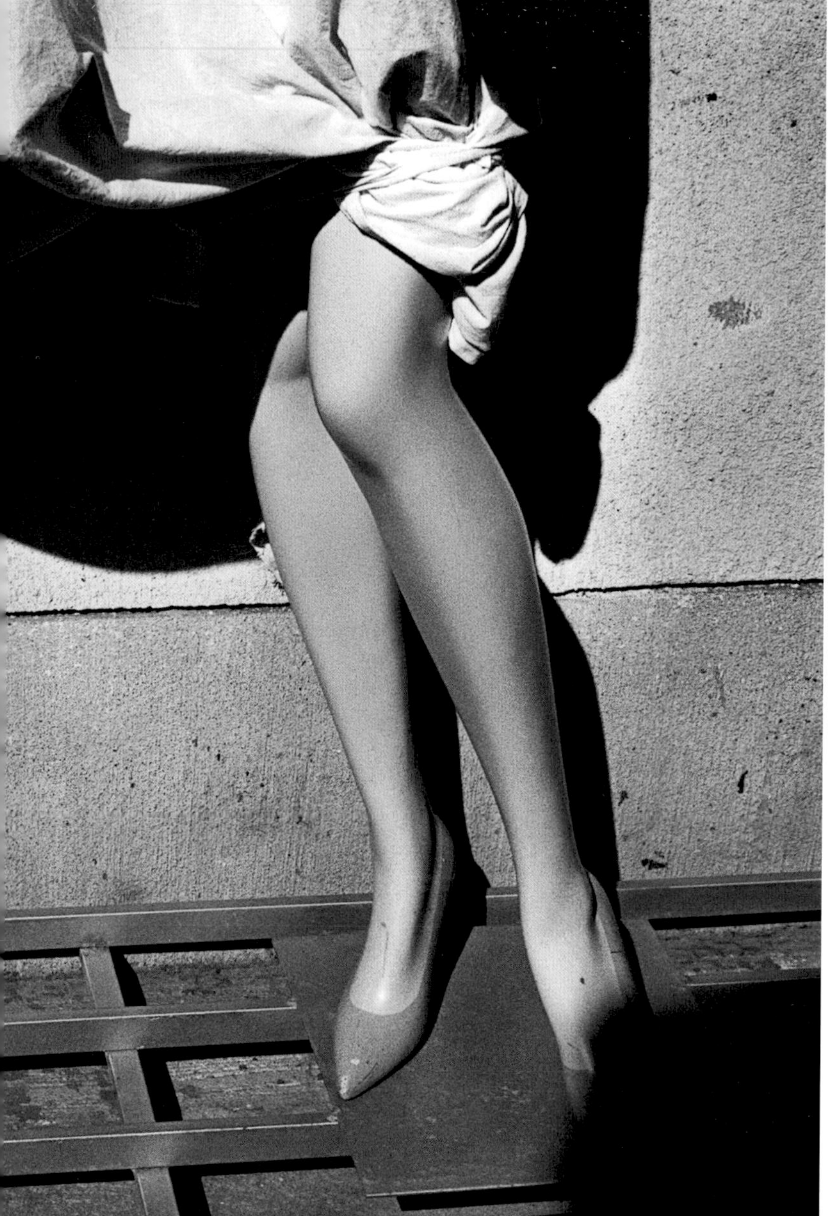

7. *Clipped*, 1972.

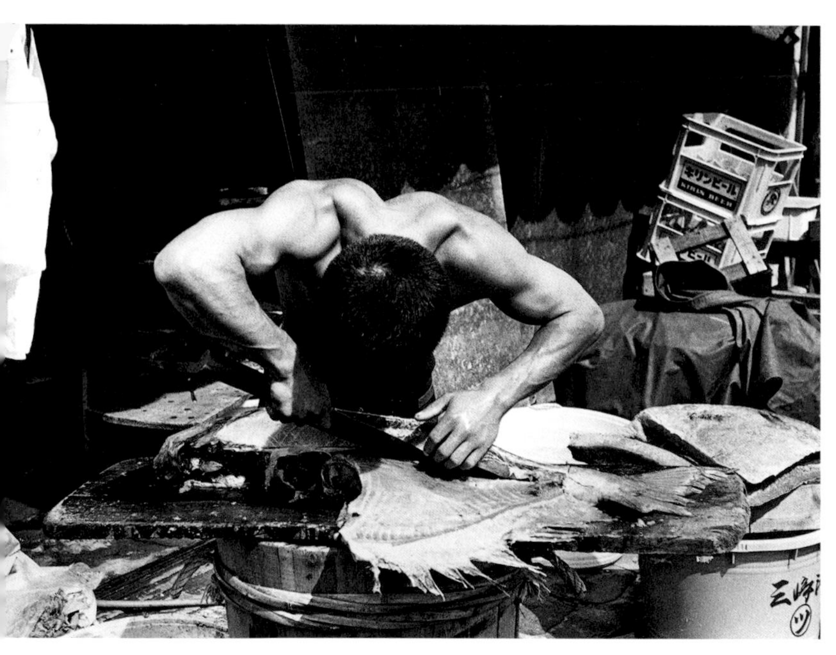

8. *Evening Shower*, 1974.

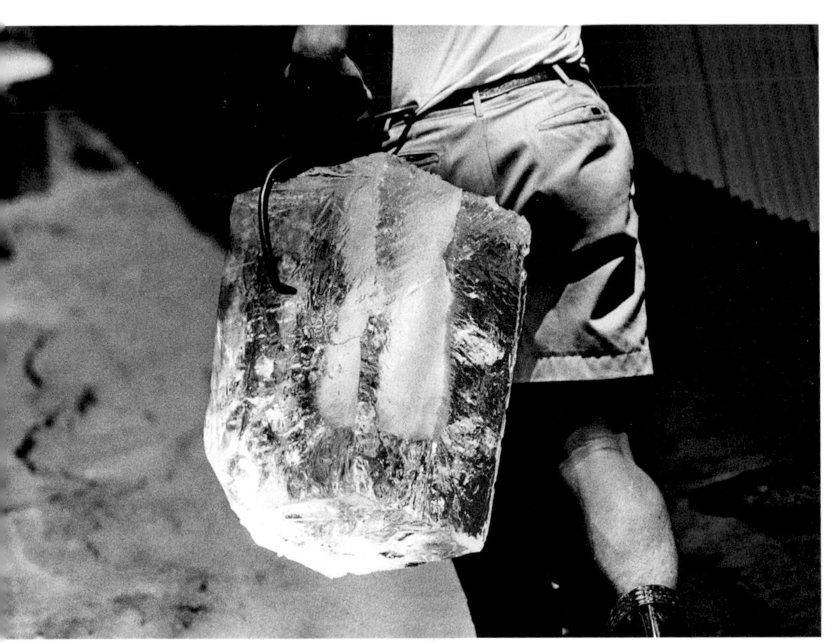

9. *Clipped*, 1972.

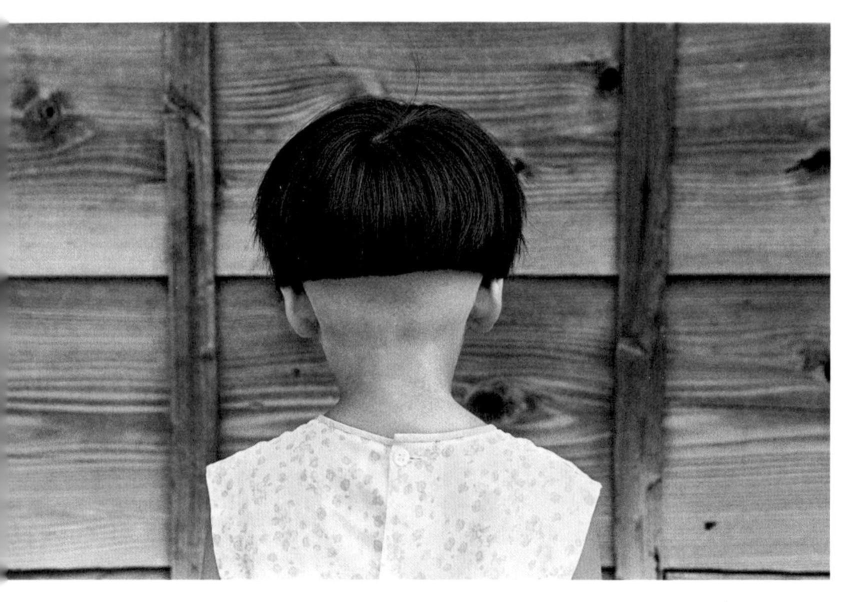

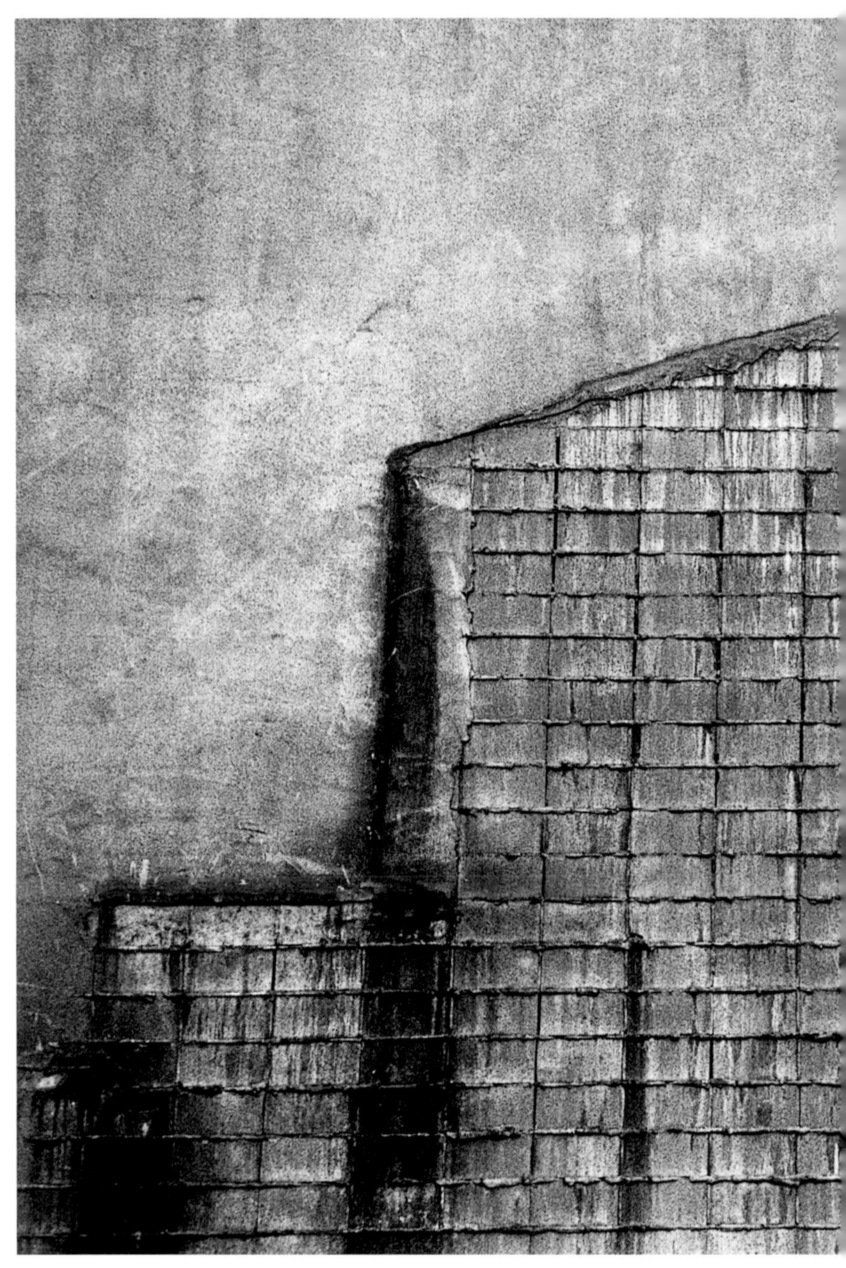

10. *Clipped*, 1972.

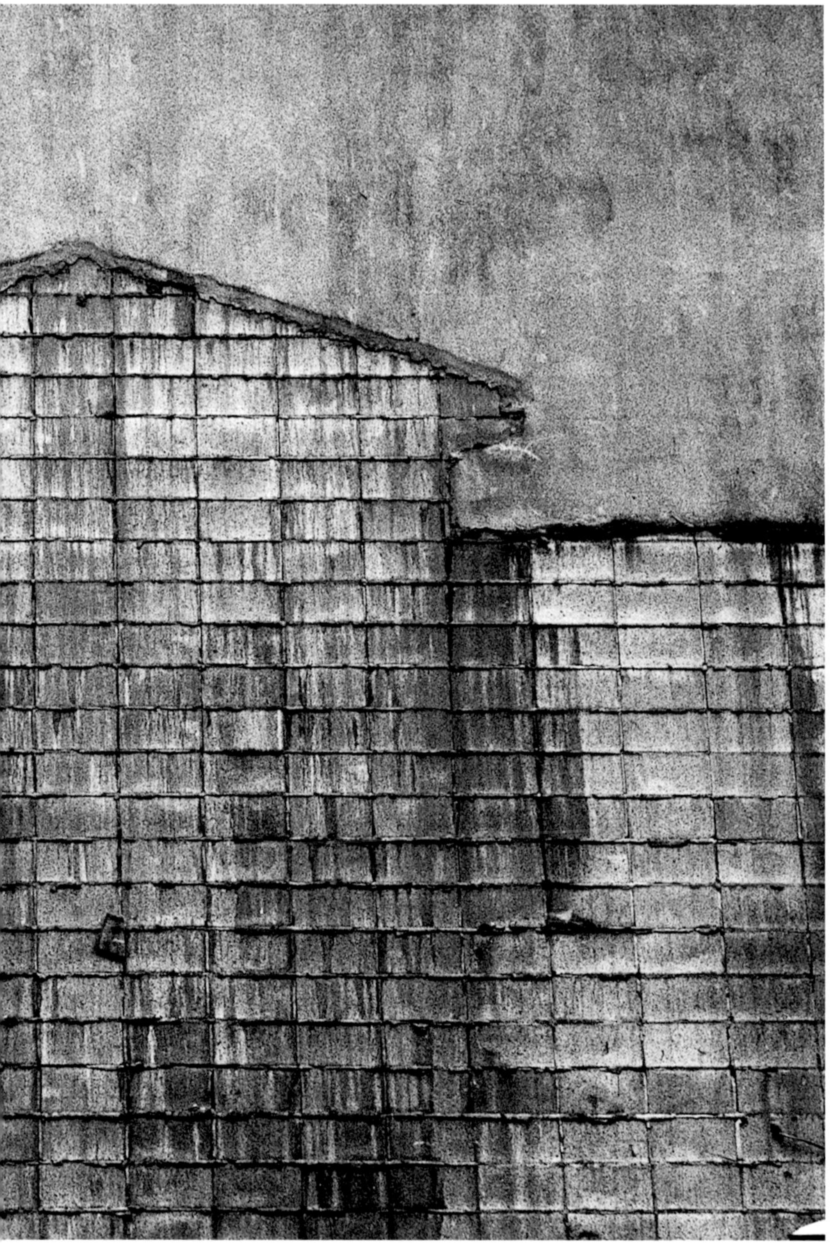

11. *Autumn Candles*, 1973.

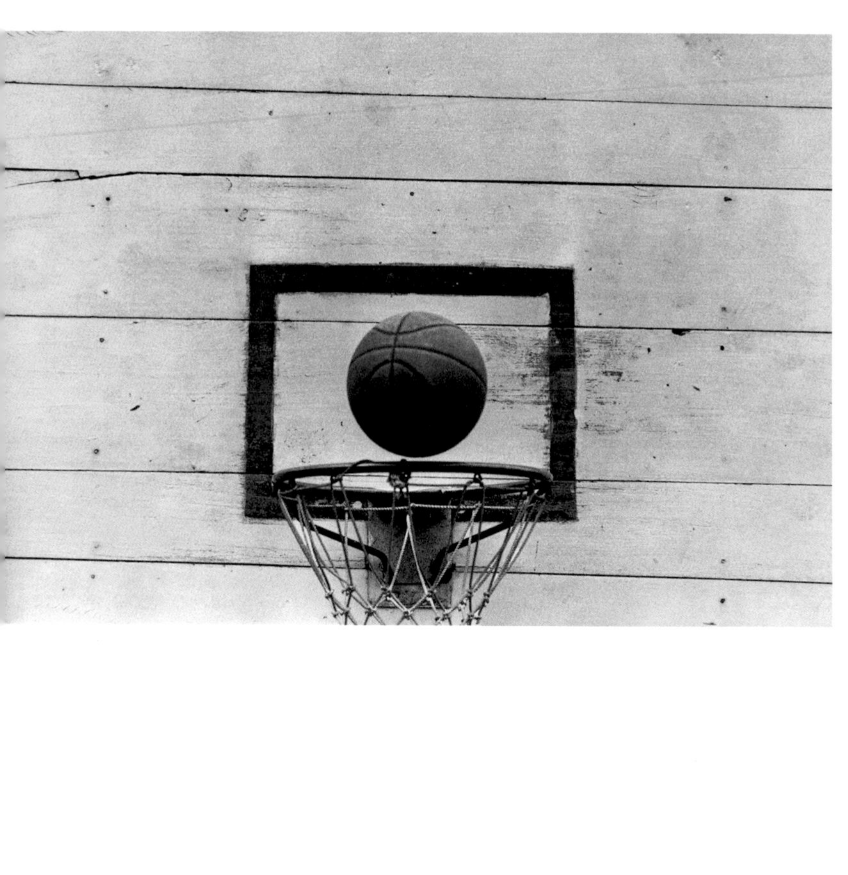

12. *Memory*, 1974.

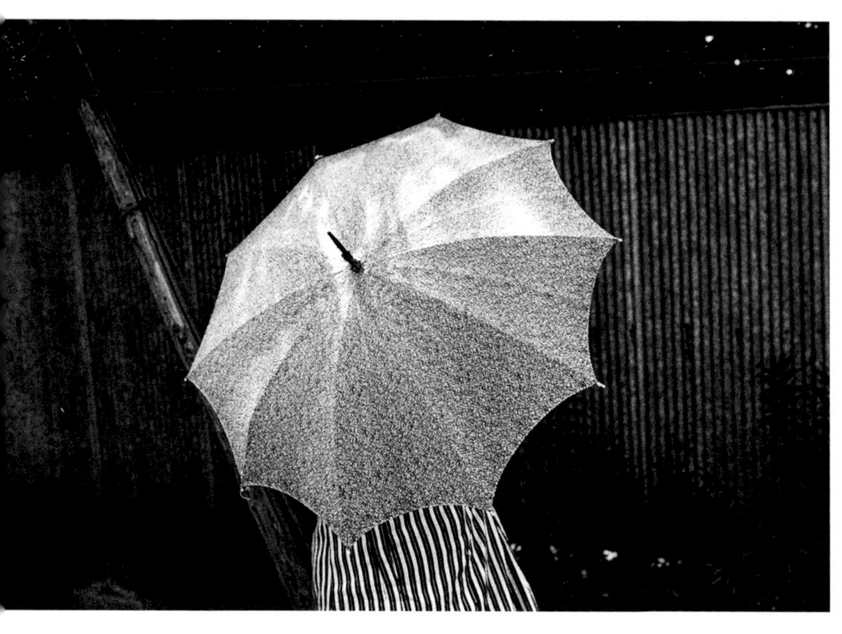

13. *Evening Shower*, early 1970s.

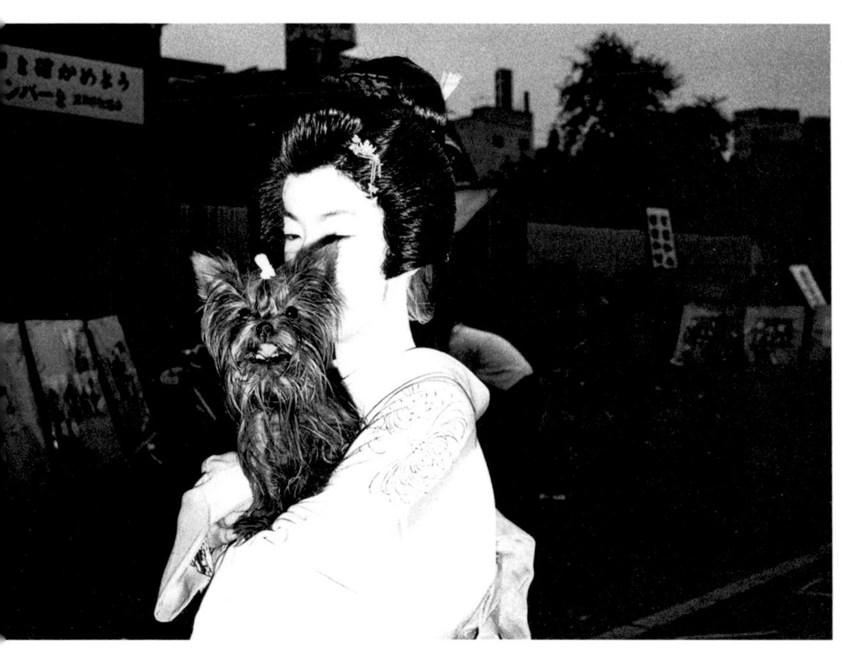

14. *Cries, At Ueno Park*, 1973.

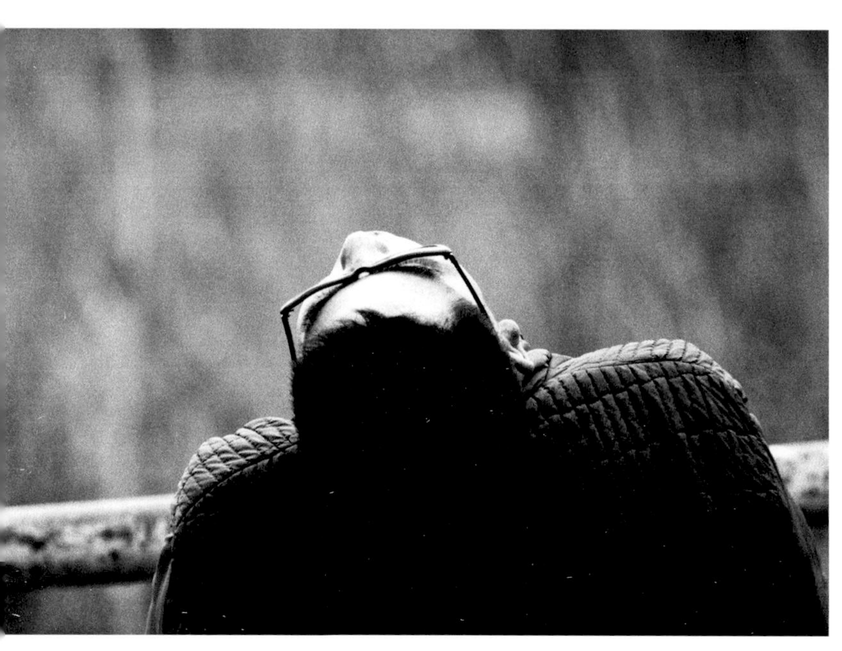

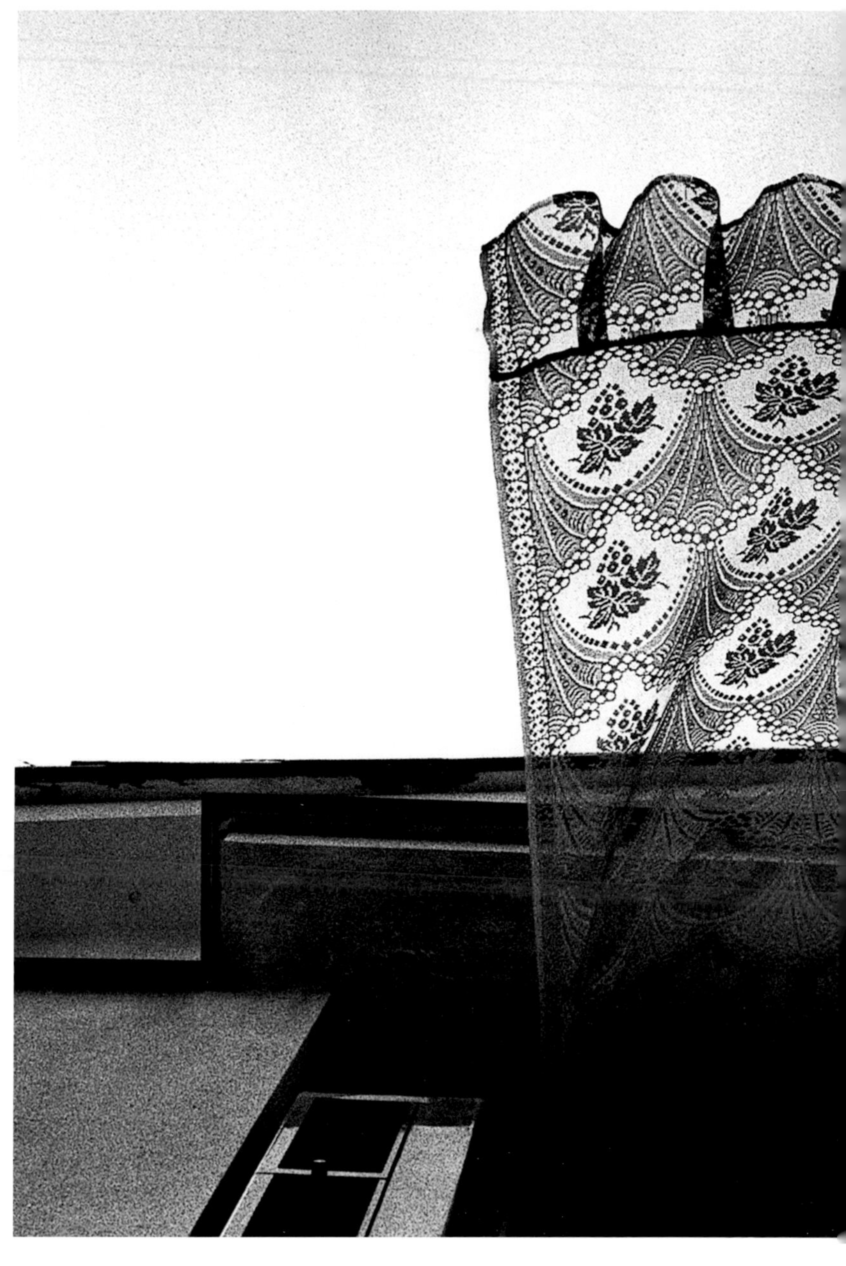

15. *Memory*, 1974.

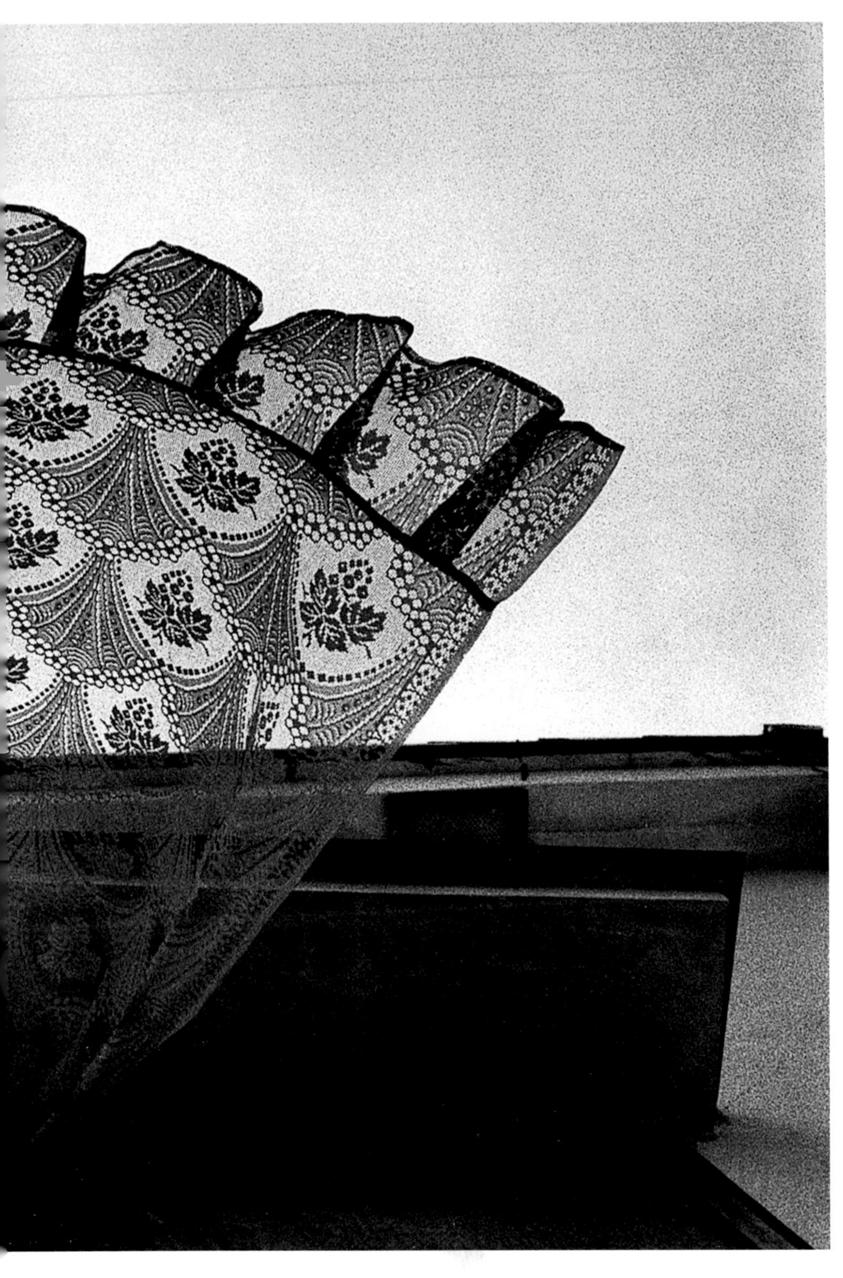

16. *Zangiku Blues*, 1972.

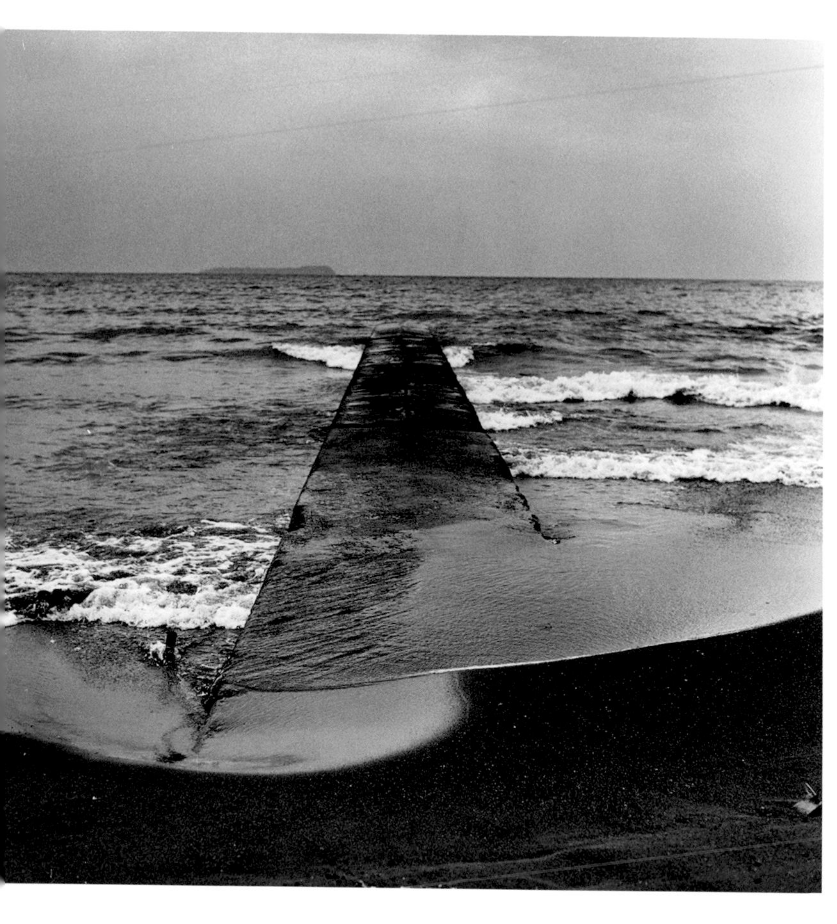

17. *Fūshi Kaden*, 1976.

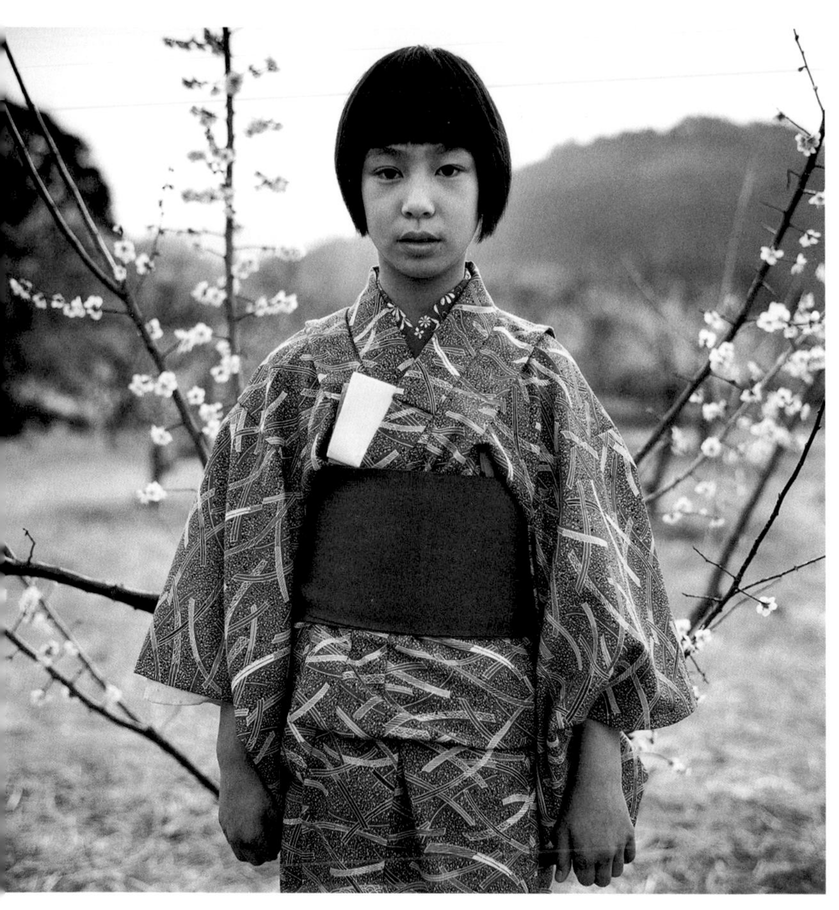

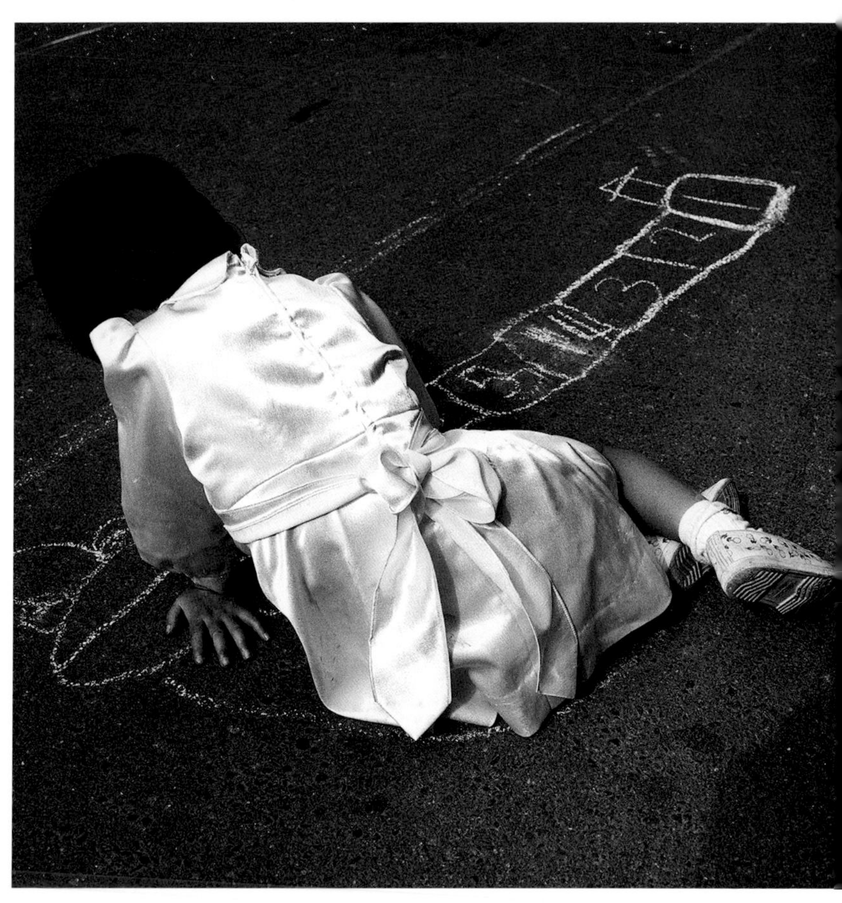

18. *Fūshi Kaden*, 1977.
19. *Fūshi Kaden*, 1975.

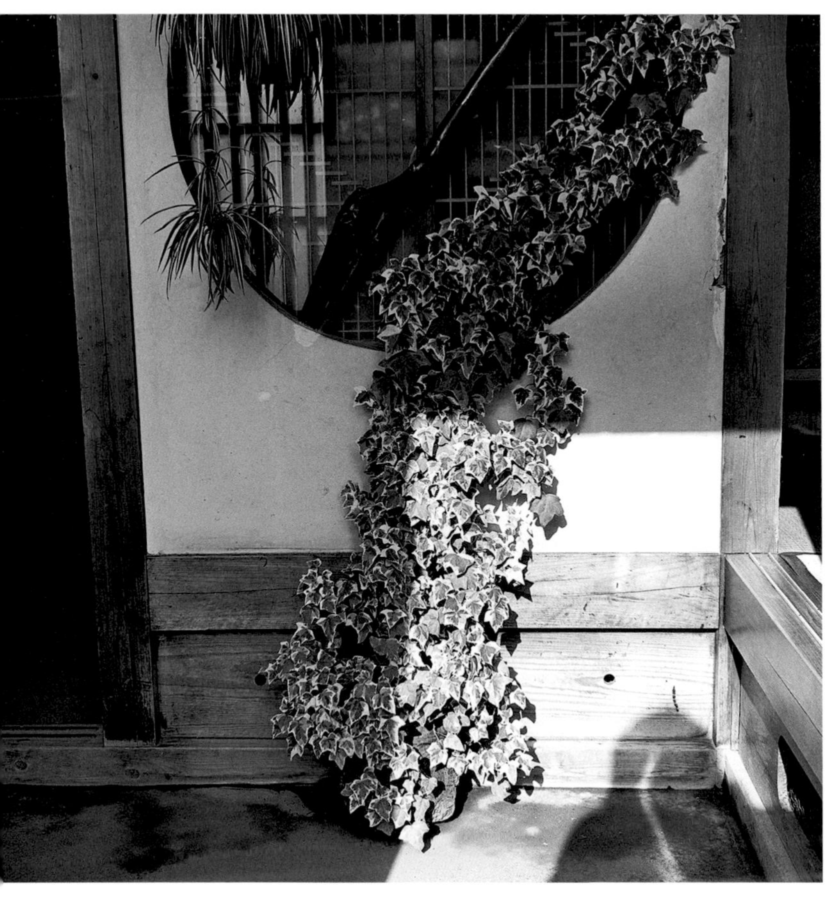

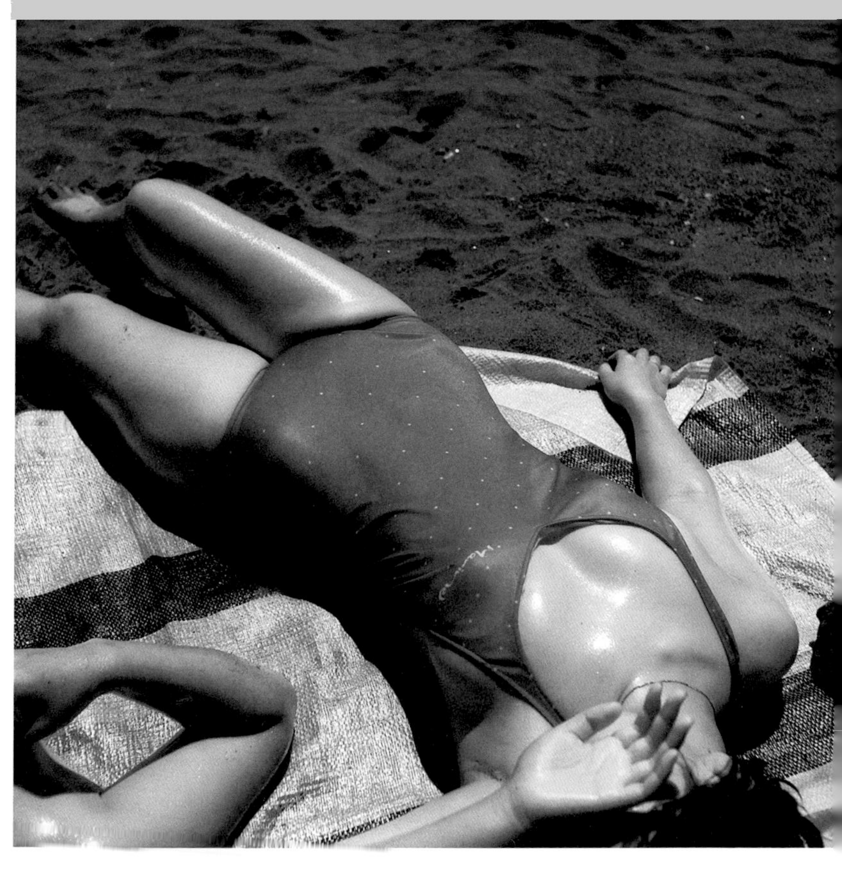

20. *Fūshi Kaden*, 1977.
21. *Fūshi Kaden*, 1975.

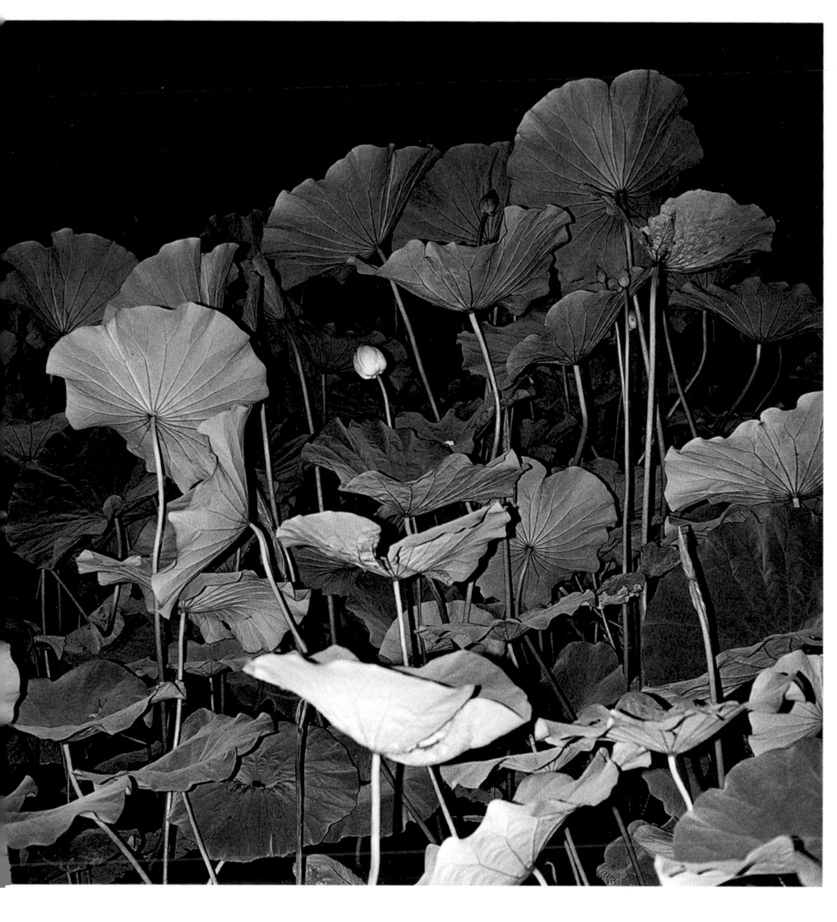

22. *Fūshi Kaden*, 1975.

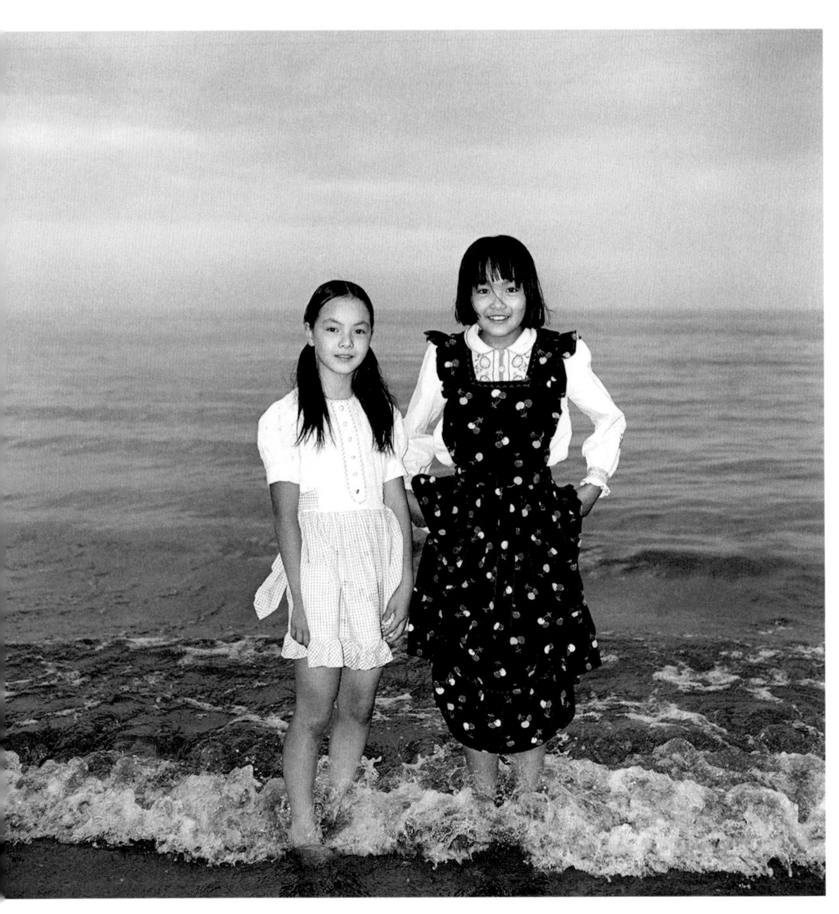

23. *Fūshi Kaden*, 1976.

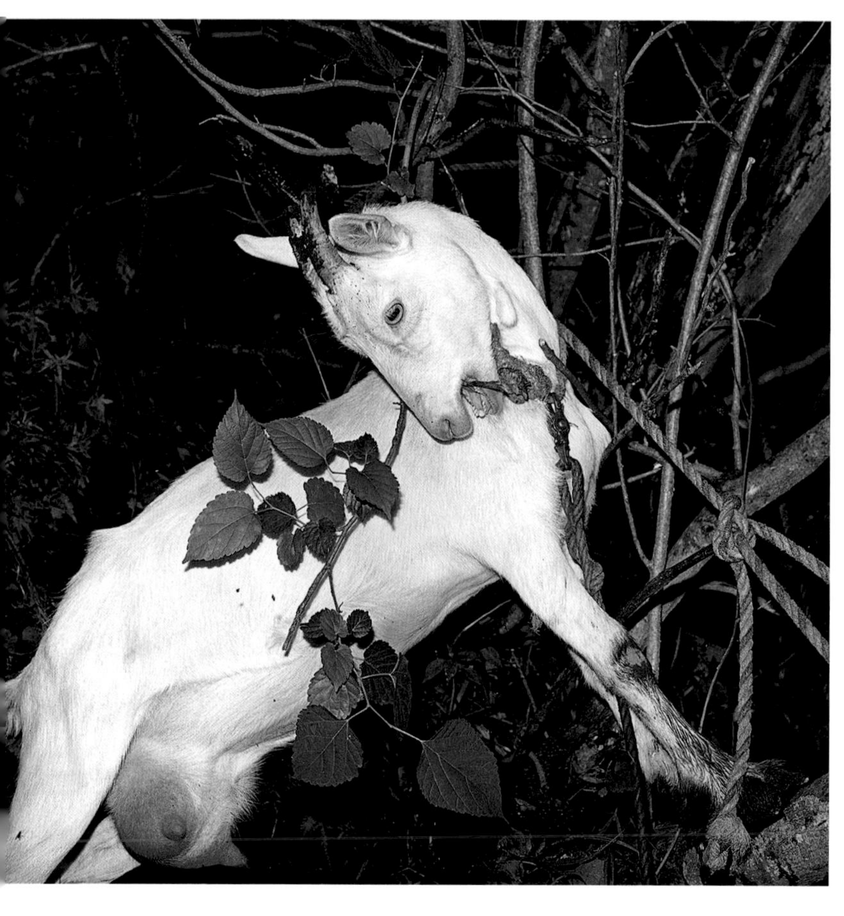

24. *Fūshi Kaden*, 1976.

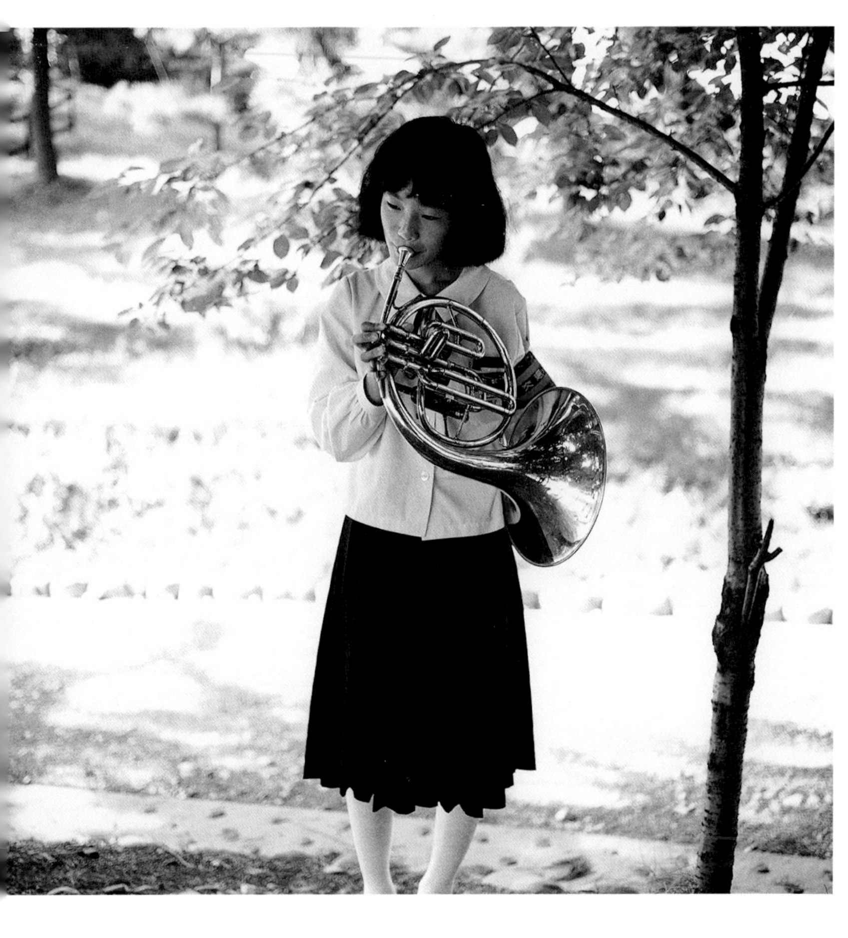

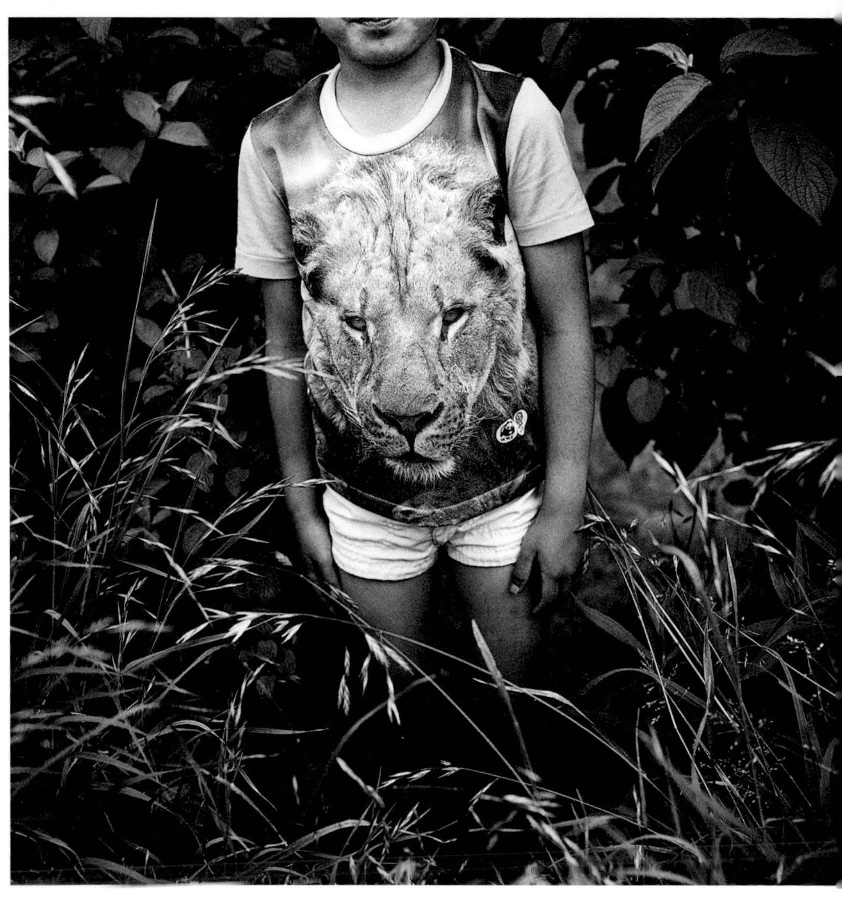

25. *Fūshi Kaden*, 1976.
26. *Fūshi Kaden*, 1977.

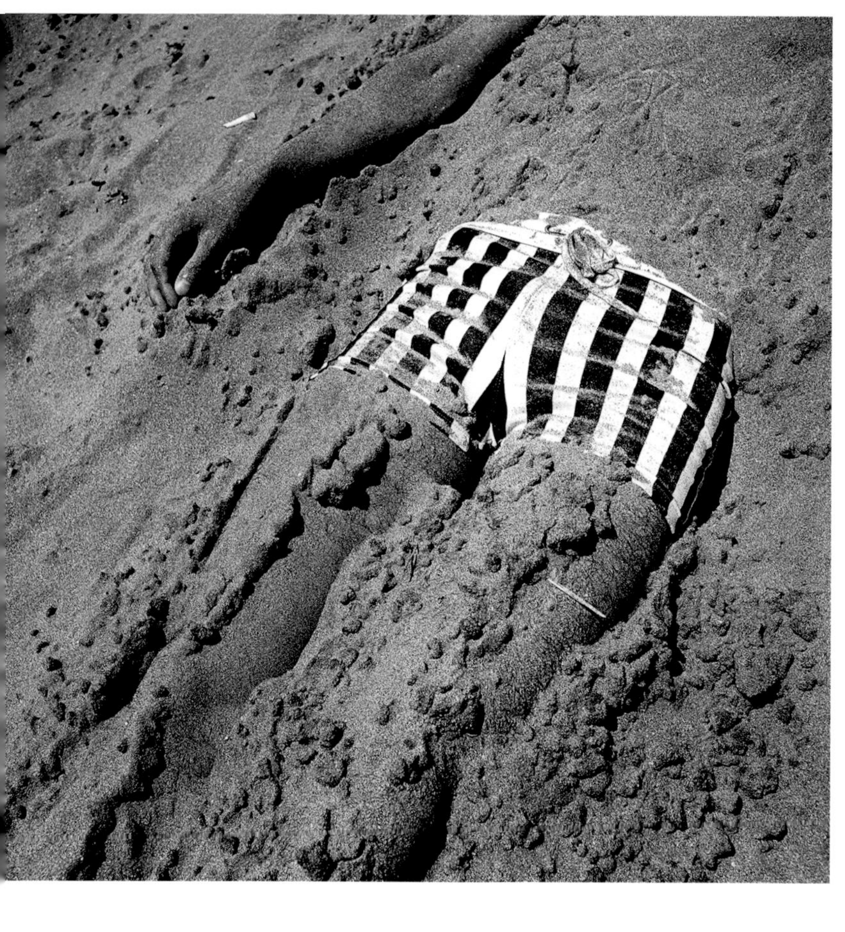

27. *Fūshi Kaden*, 1976.

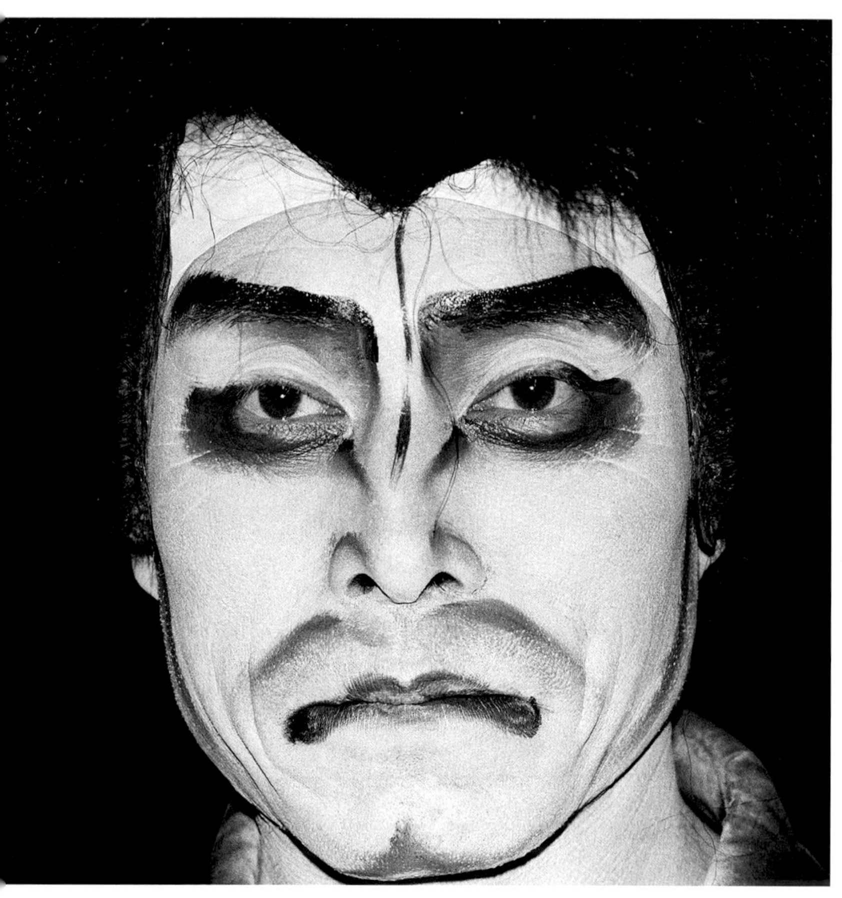

28. *Fūshi Kaden*, 1976.

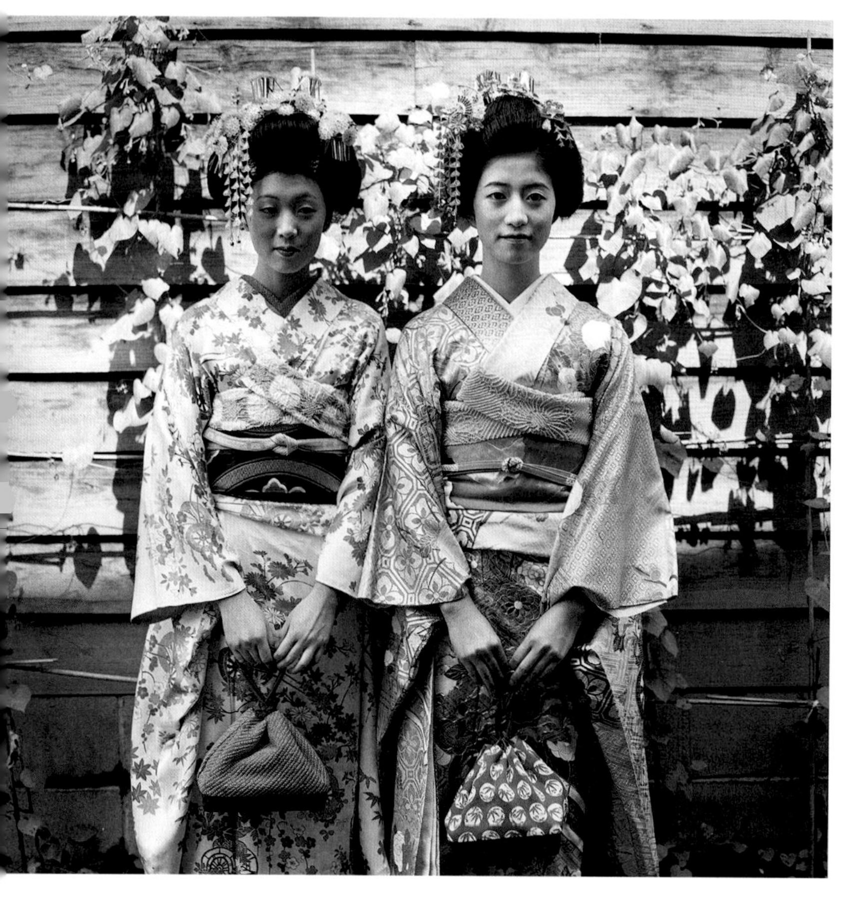

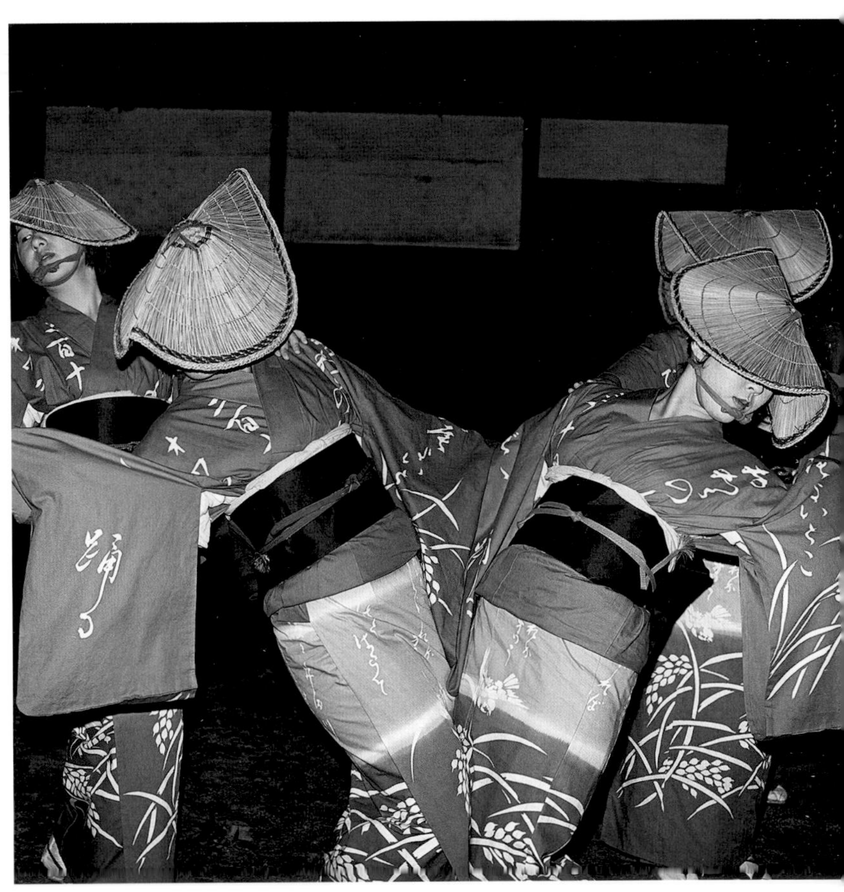

29. *Fūshi Kaden*, 1976.
30. *Fūshi Kaden*, 1975.

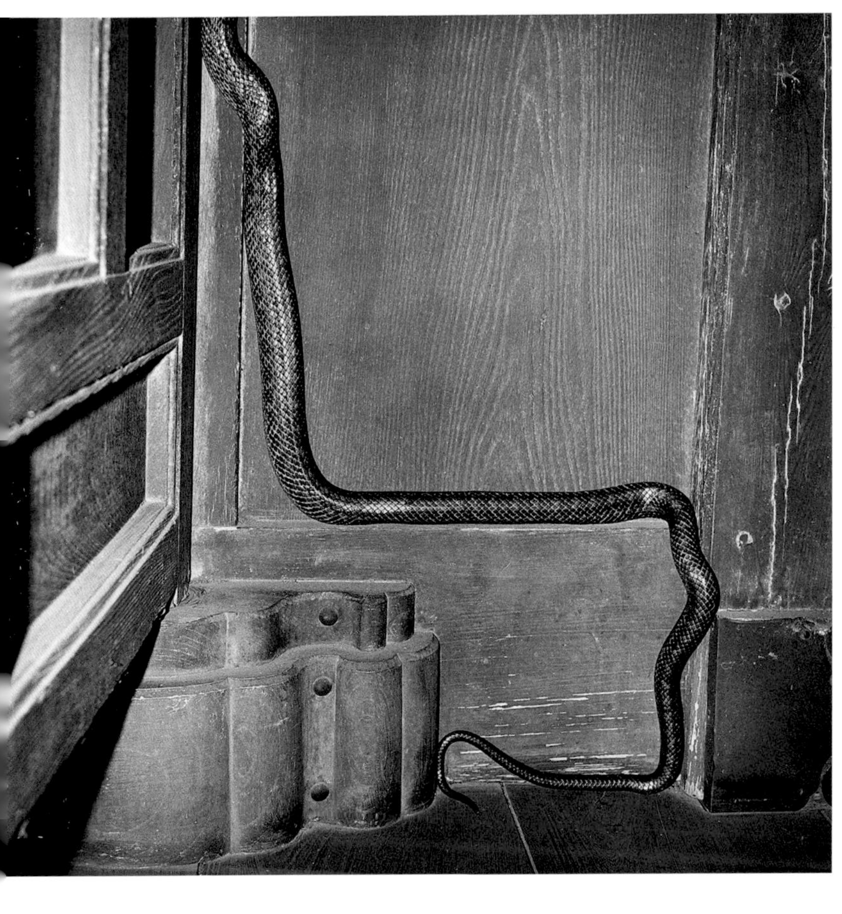

31. *Fūshi Kaden*, 1976.

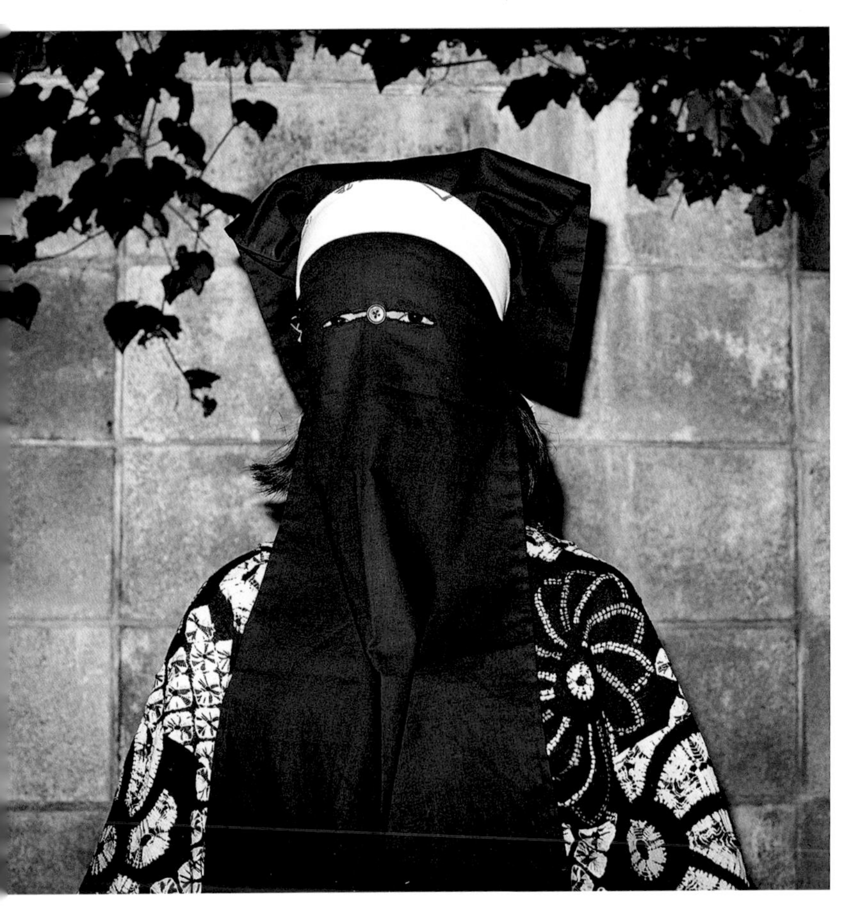

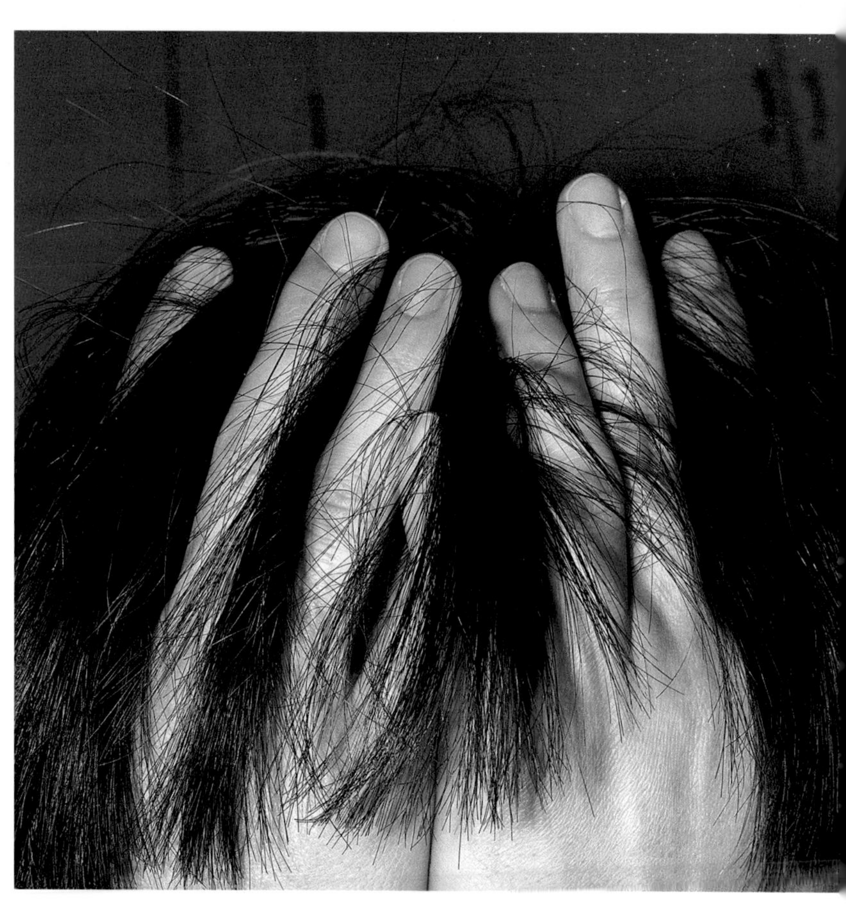

32. *Fūshi Kaden*, 1975.
33. *Fūshi Kaden*, 1976.

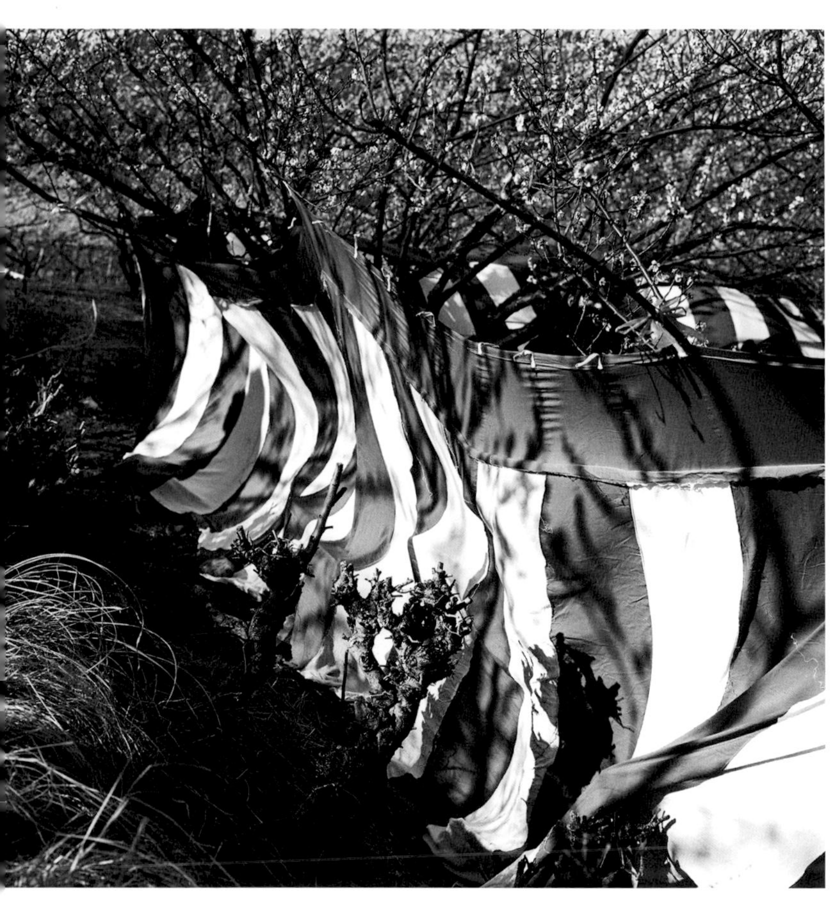

34. *78*, 1977.

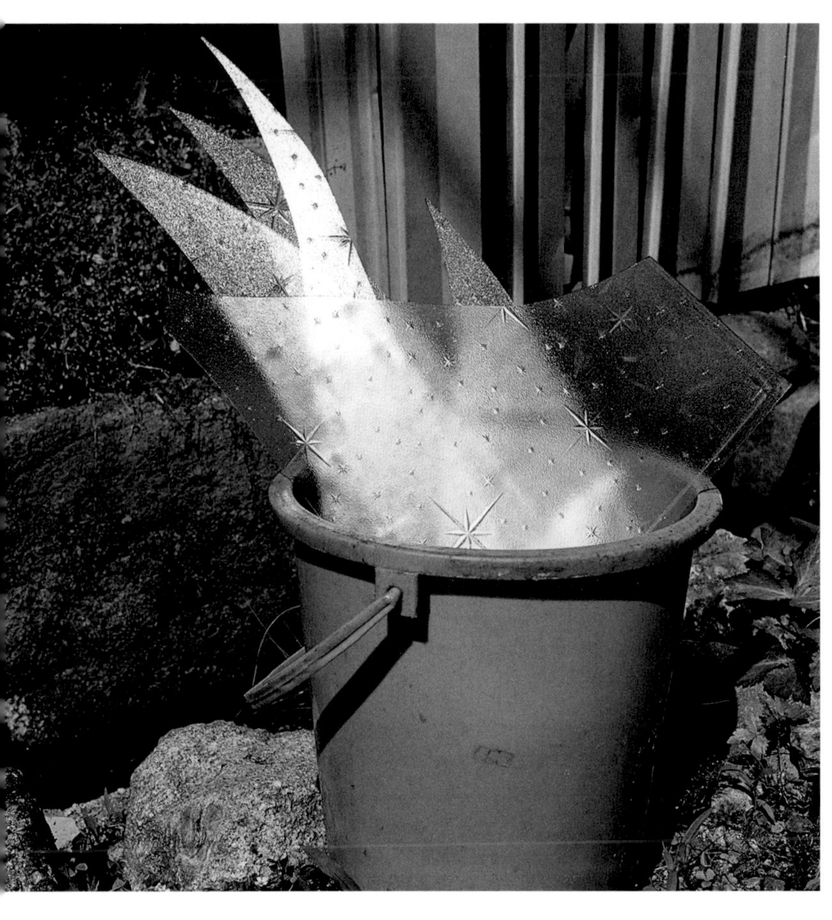

35. *The Sketch of Kanto Area*, 1983.

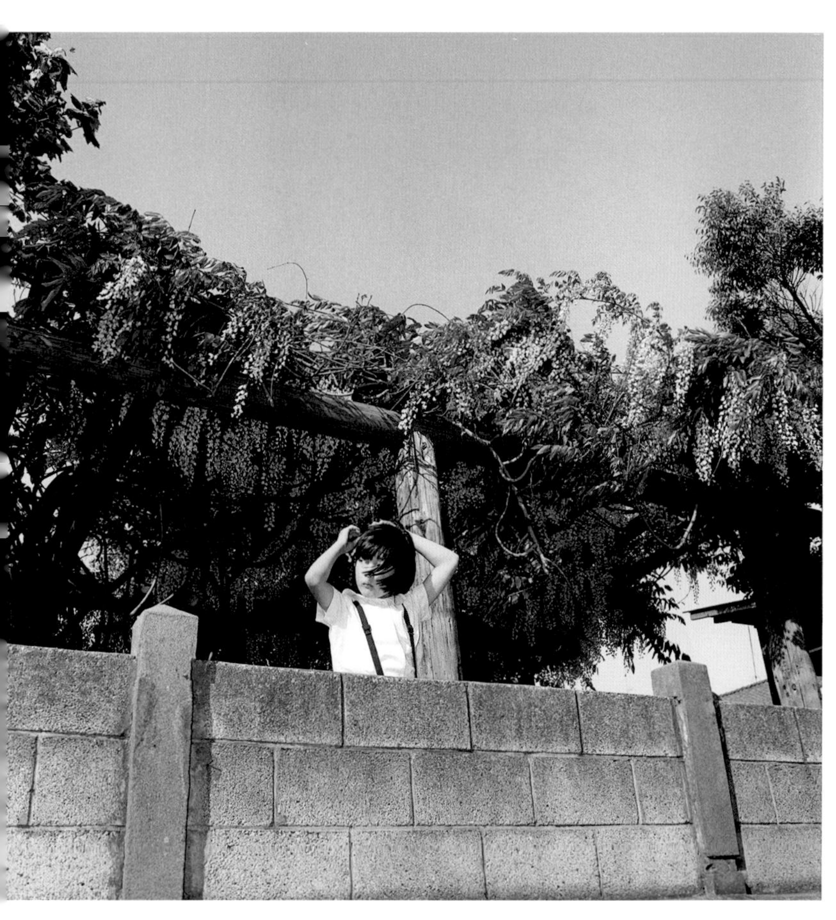

36. *Childhood Days*, 1975.

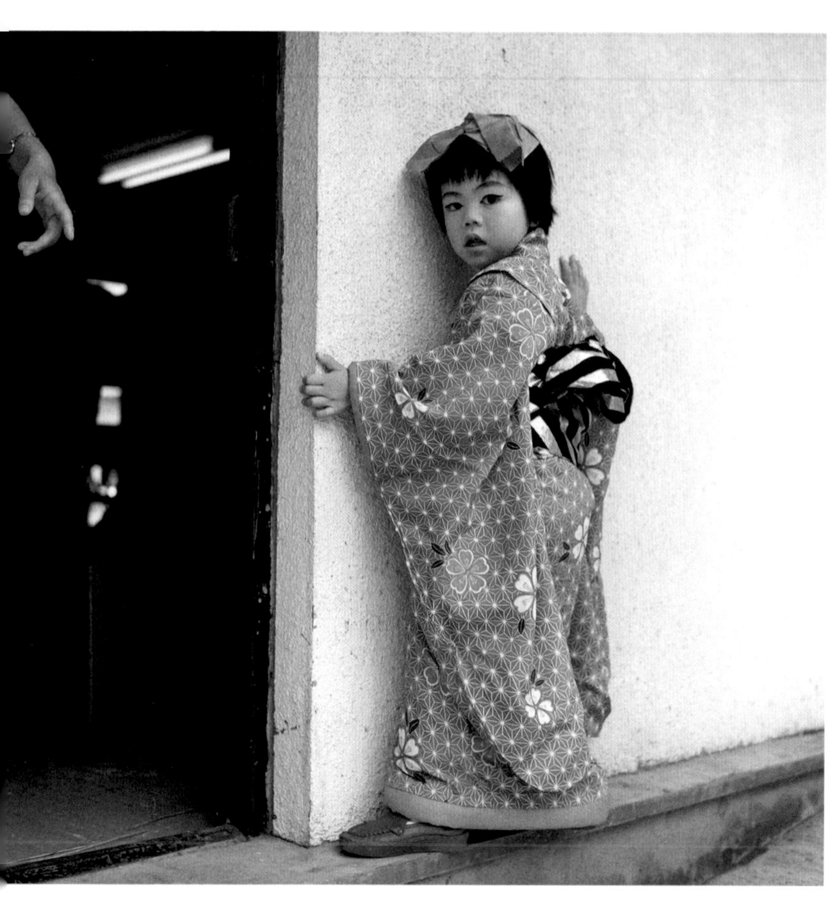

37. *Childhood Days*, 1972.

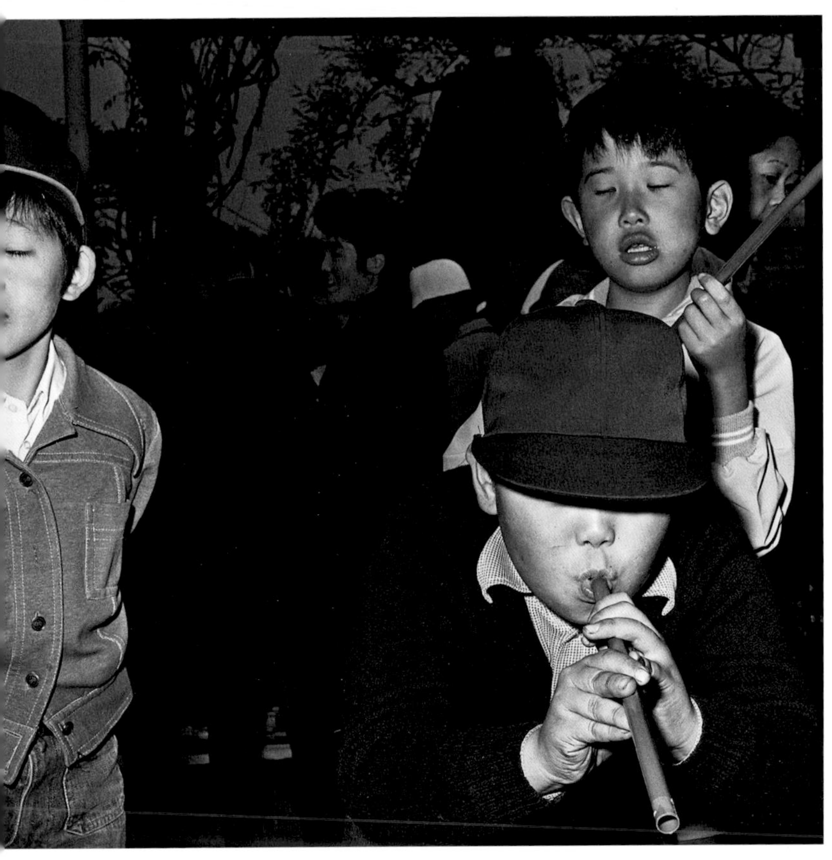

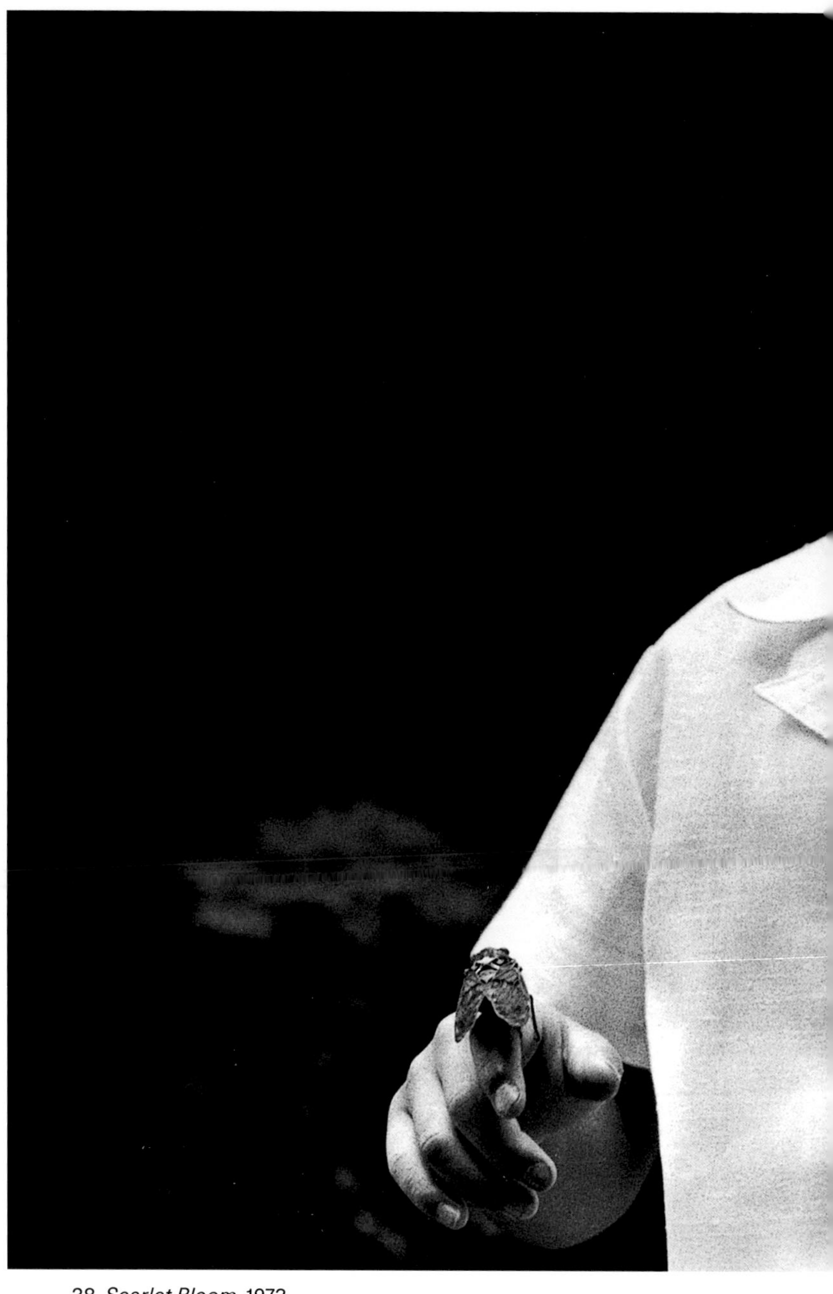

38. *Scarlet Bloom*, 1972.

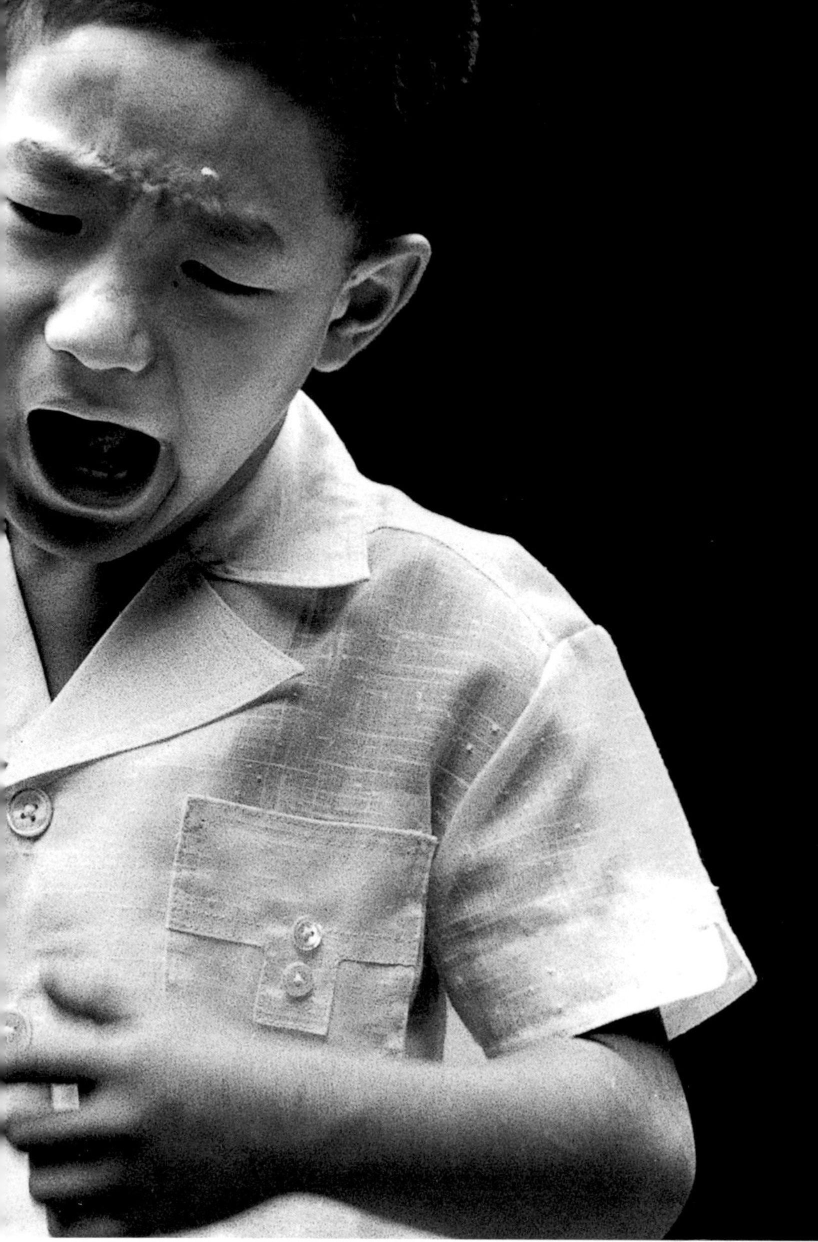

39. *Childhood Days*, 1982.

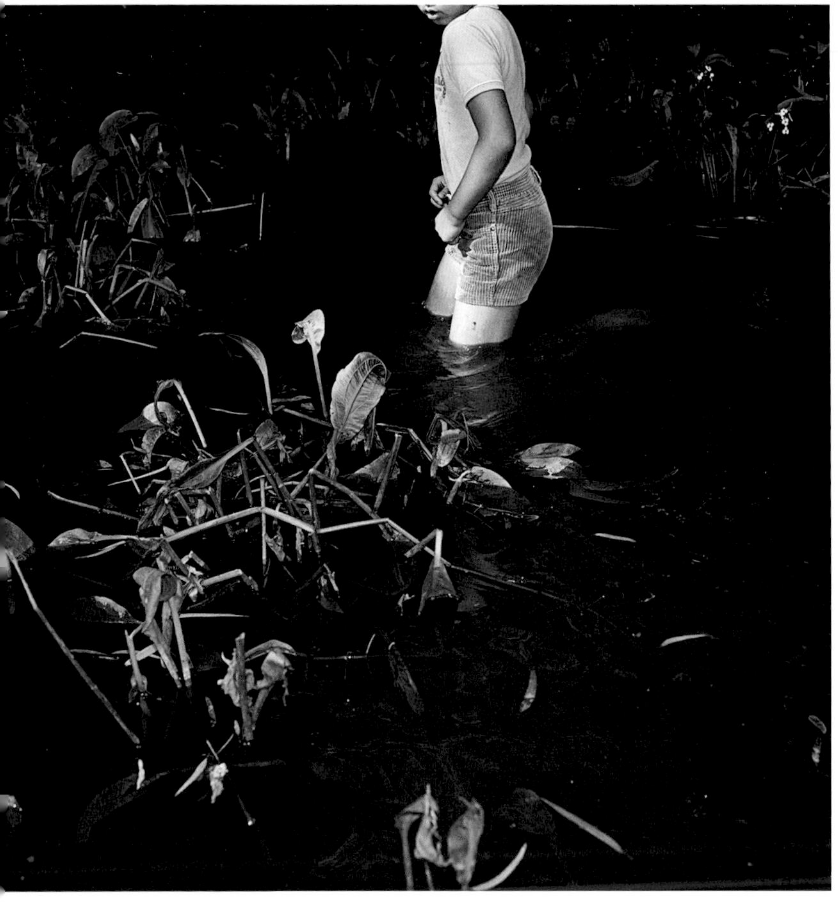

40. *Anonymous Man and Woman*, 1977.

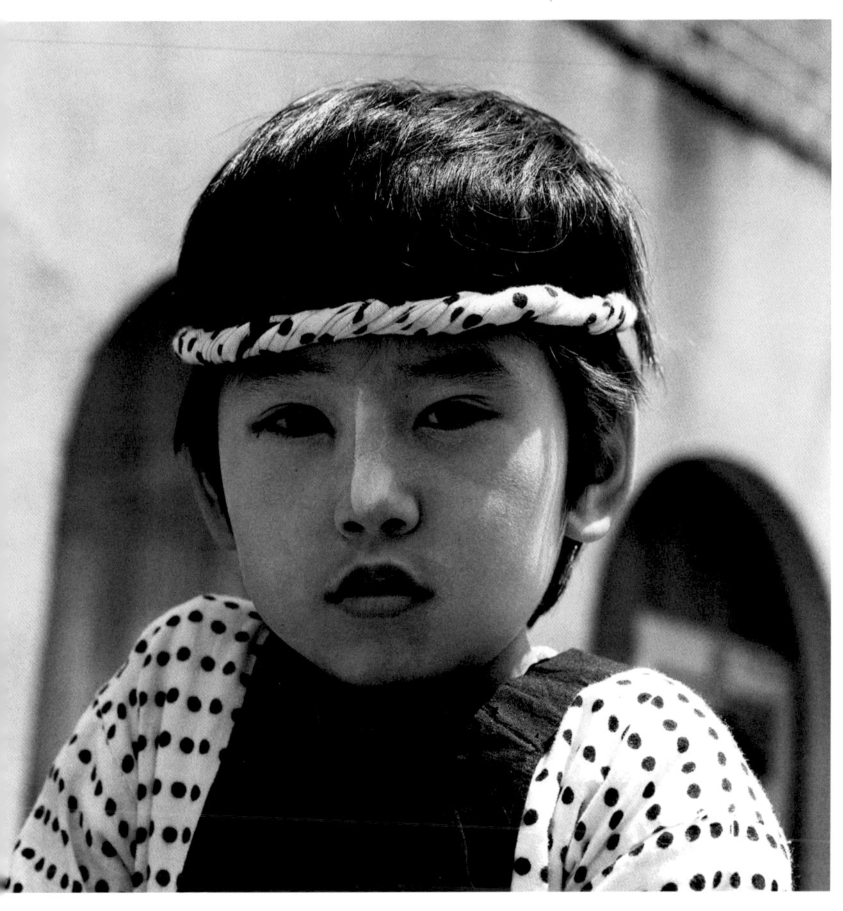

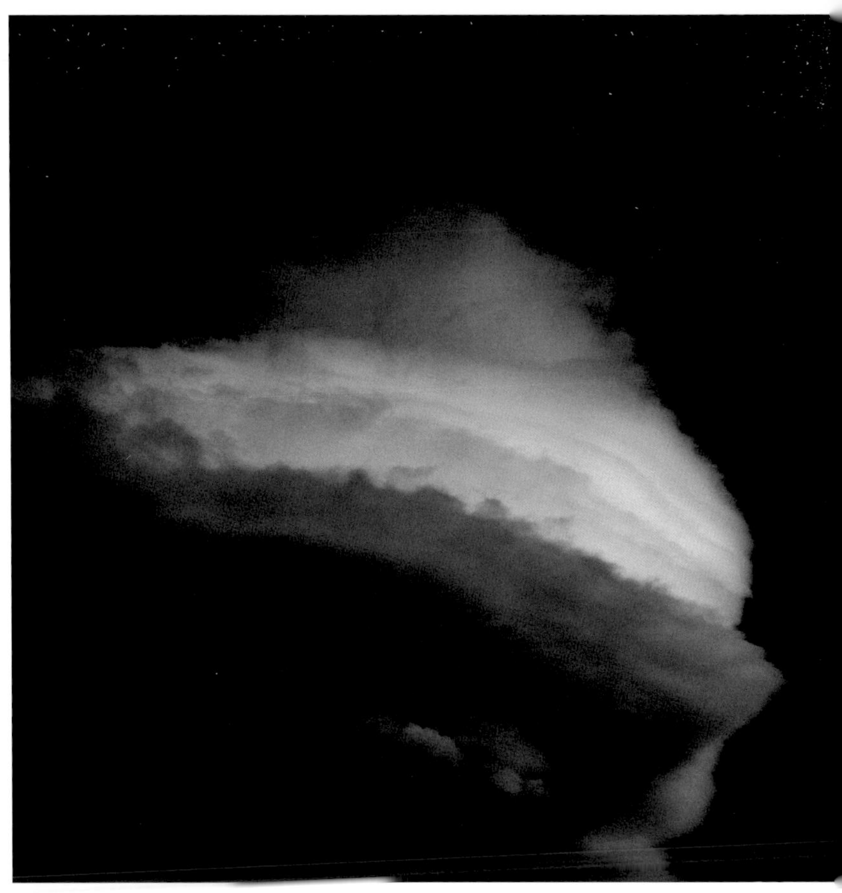

41. *Scarlet Bloom*, 1972.
42. *Childhood Days*, 1978.

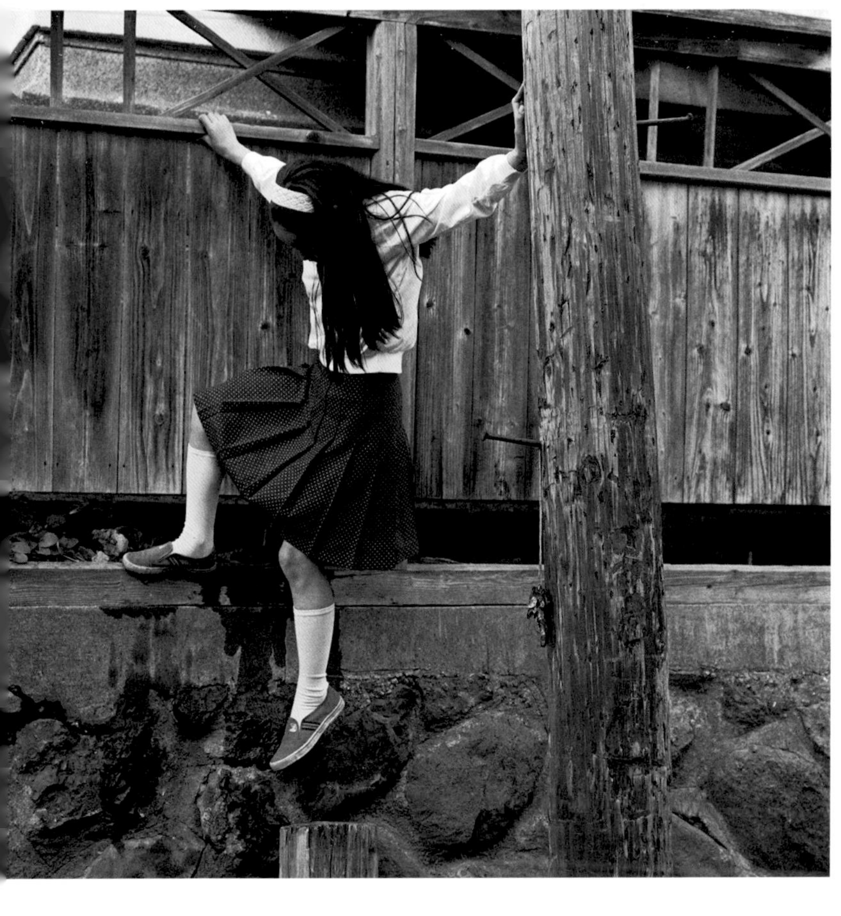

43. *Scarlet Bloom*, 1973.

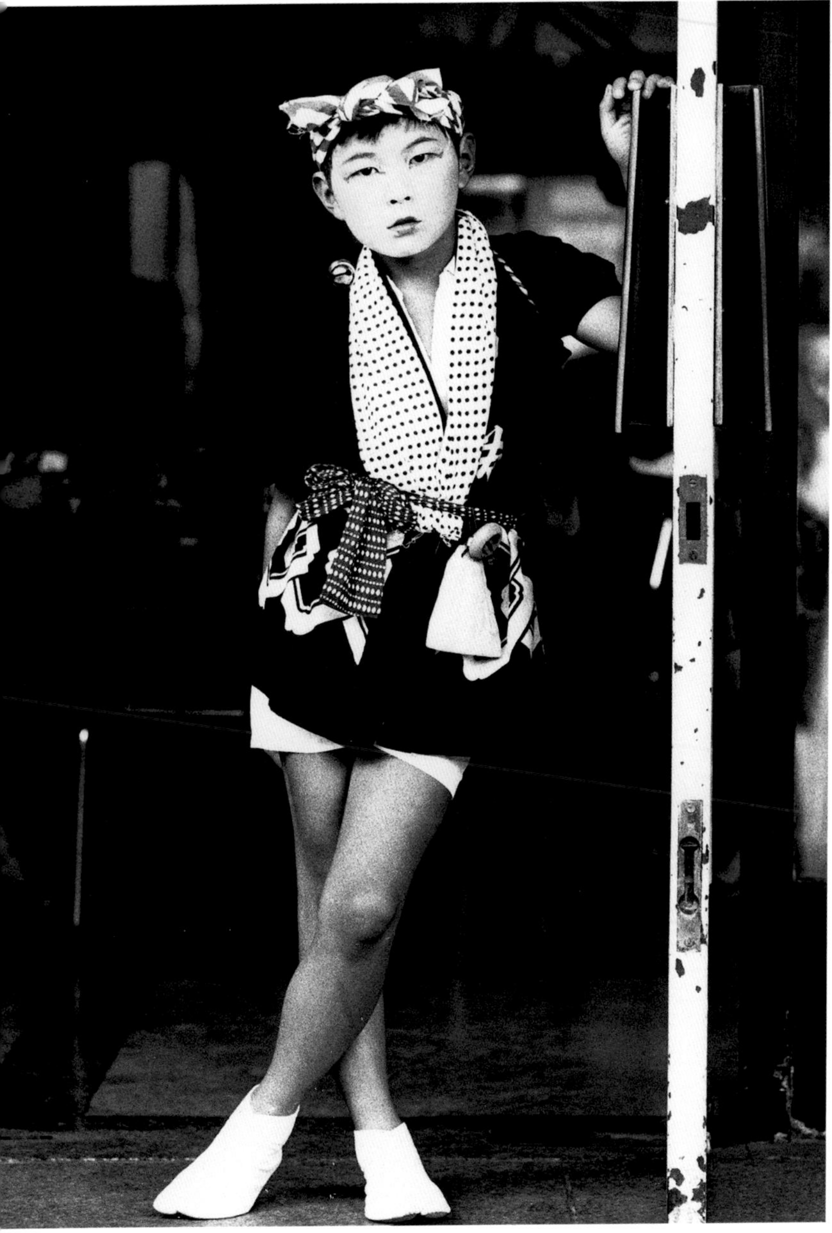

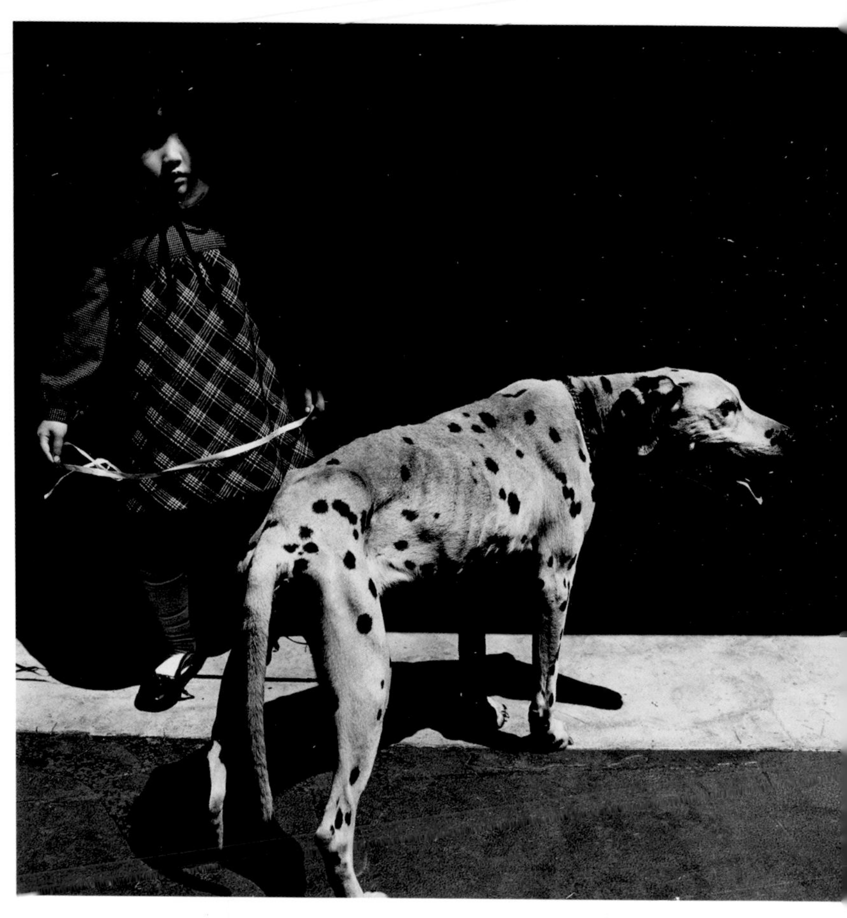

44. *Childhood Days*, 1981.
45. *Monogusa Shui*, 1980.

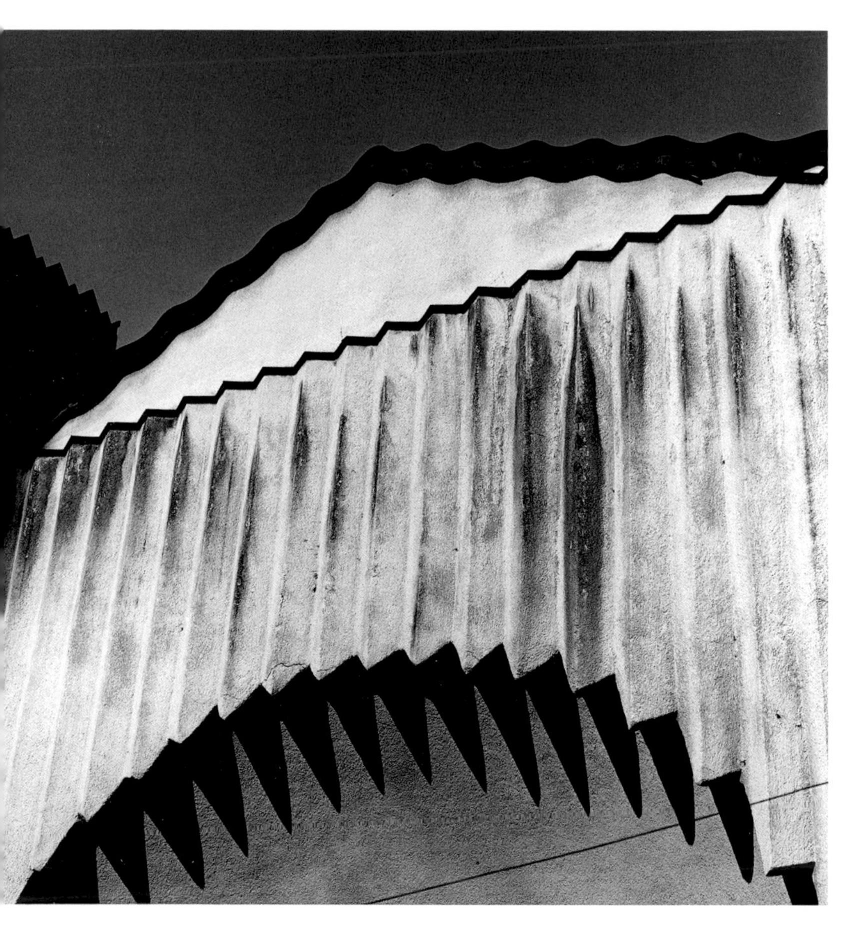

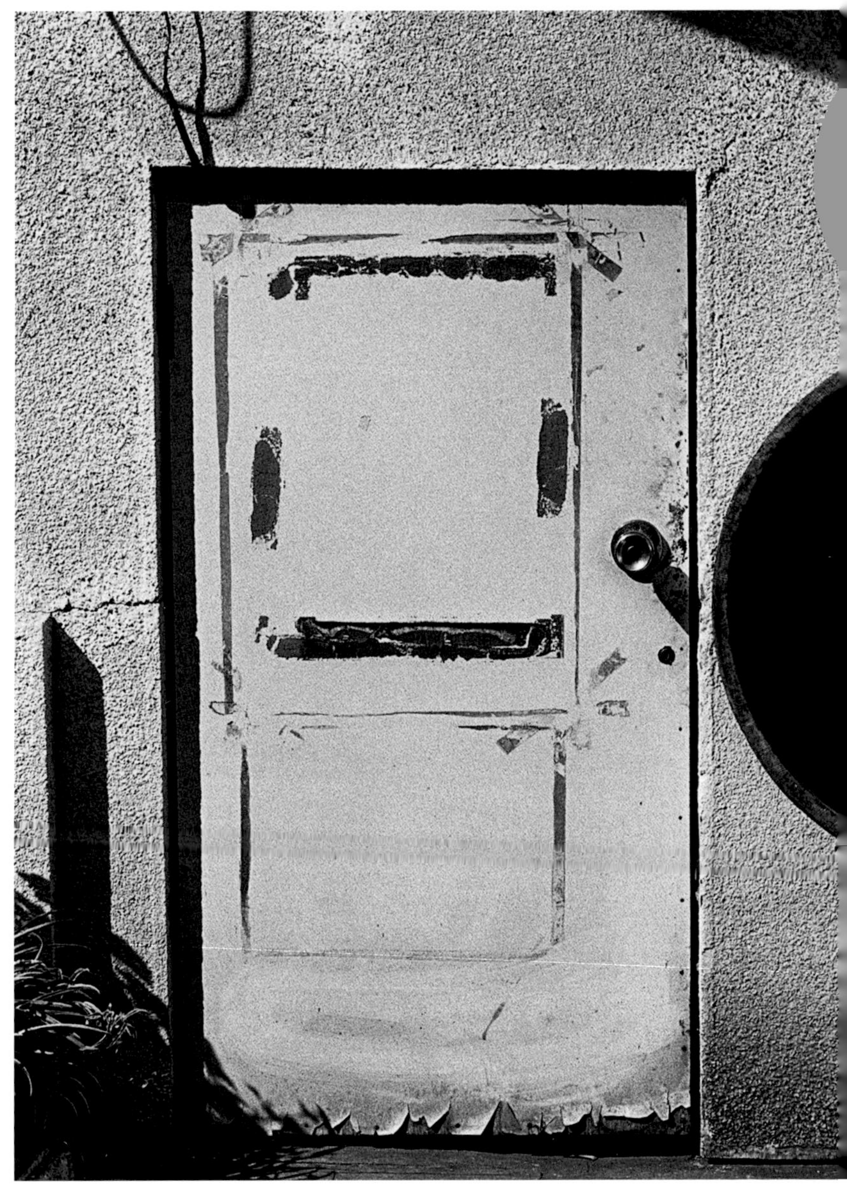

46. *Journey to the Tobacco Shop on the Corner*, 1979.

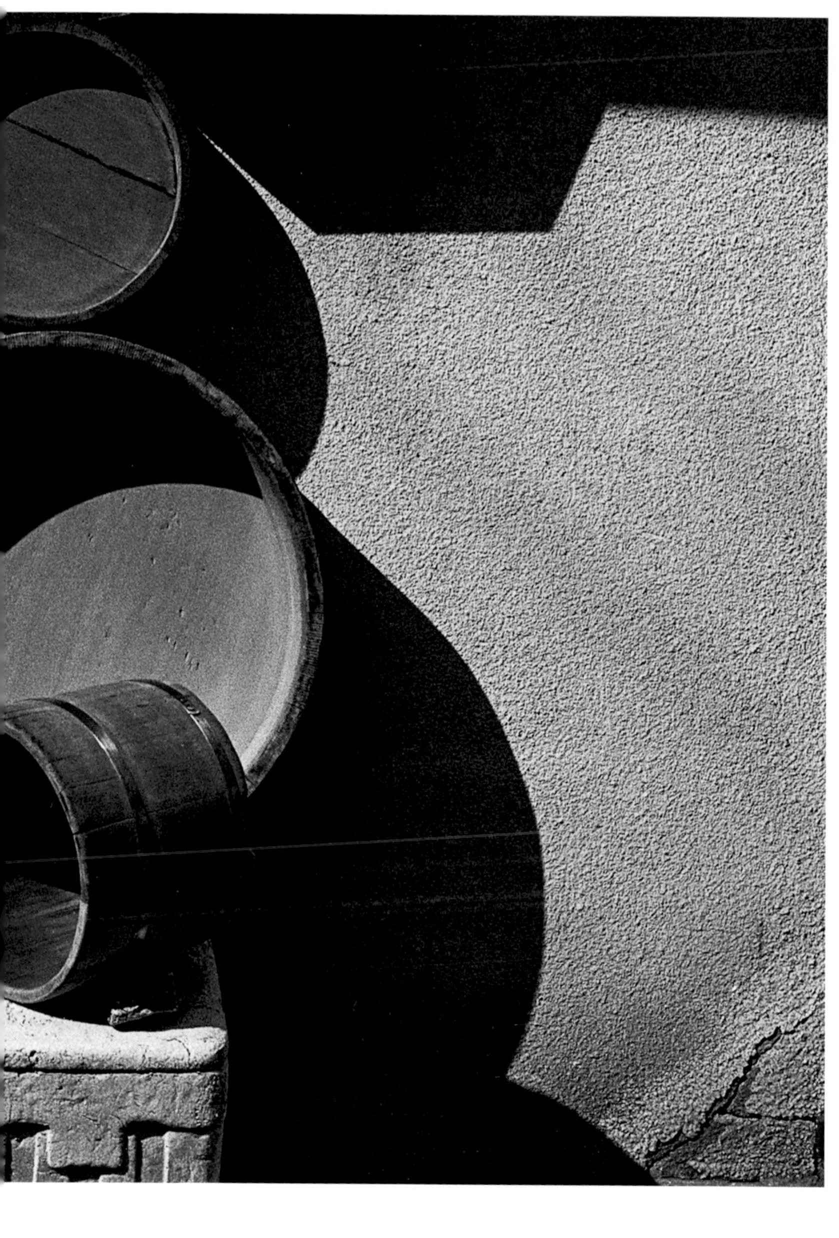

47. *Monogusa Shui*, 1981.

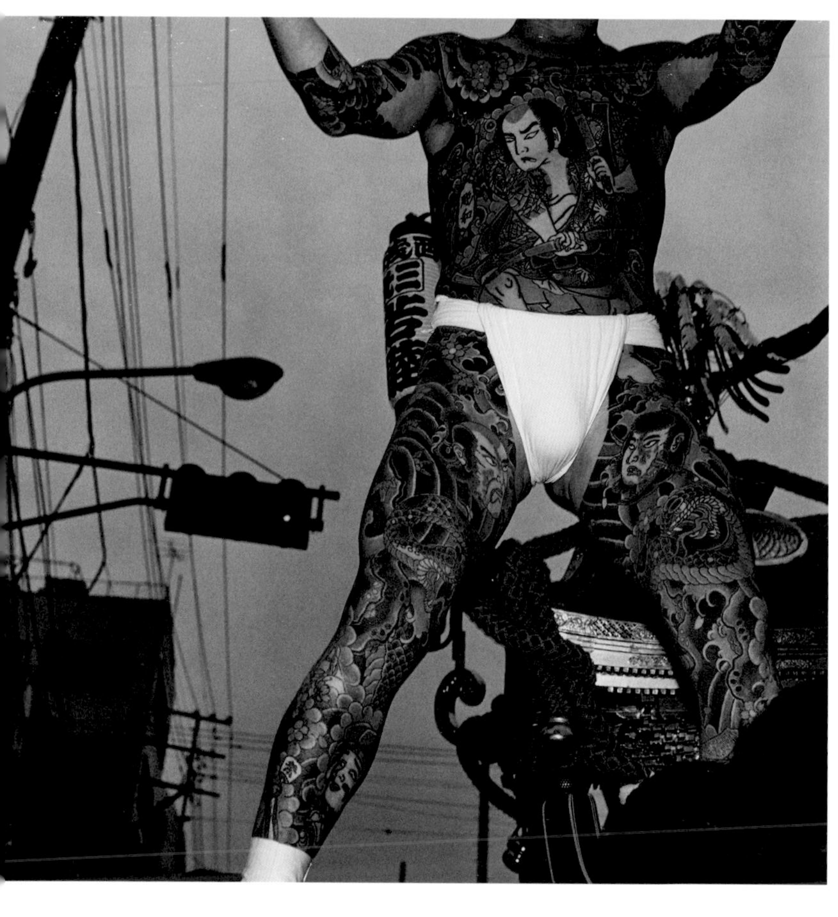

48. *Anonymous Man and Woman*, 1977.

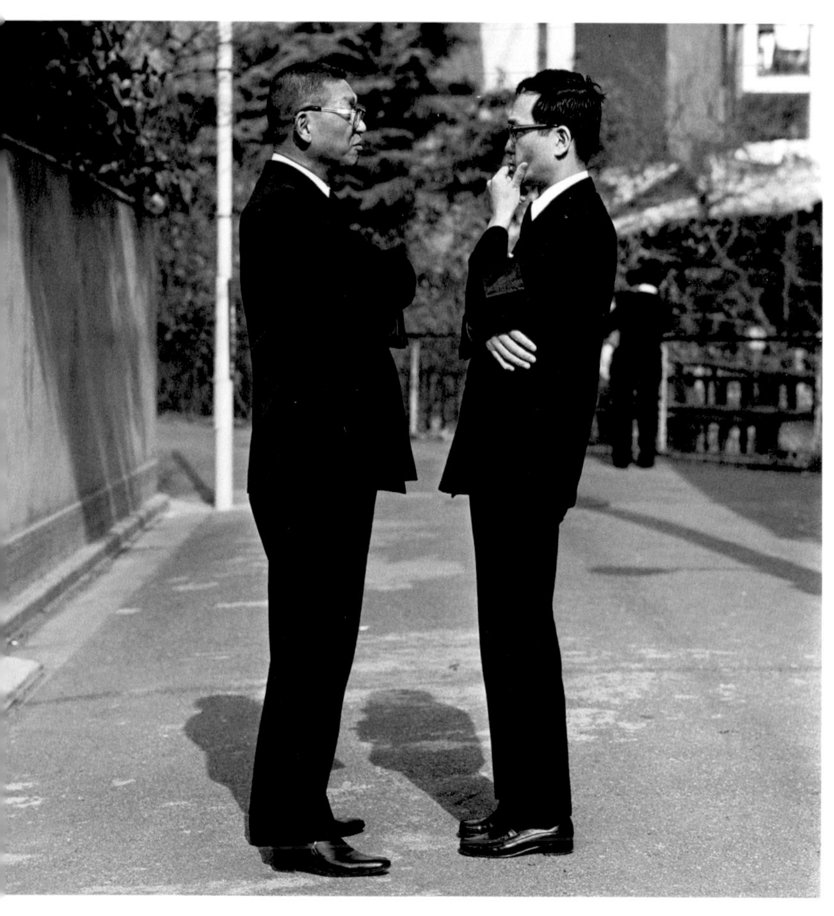

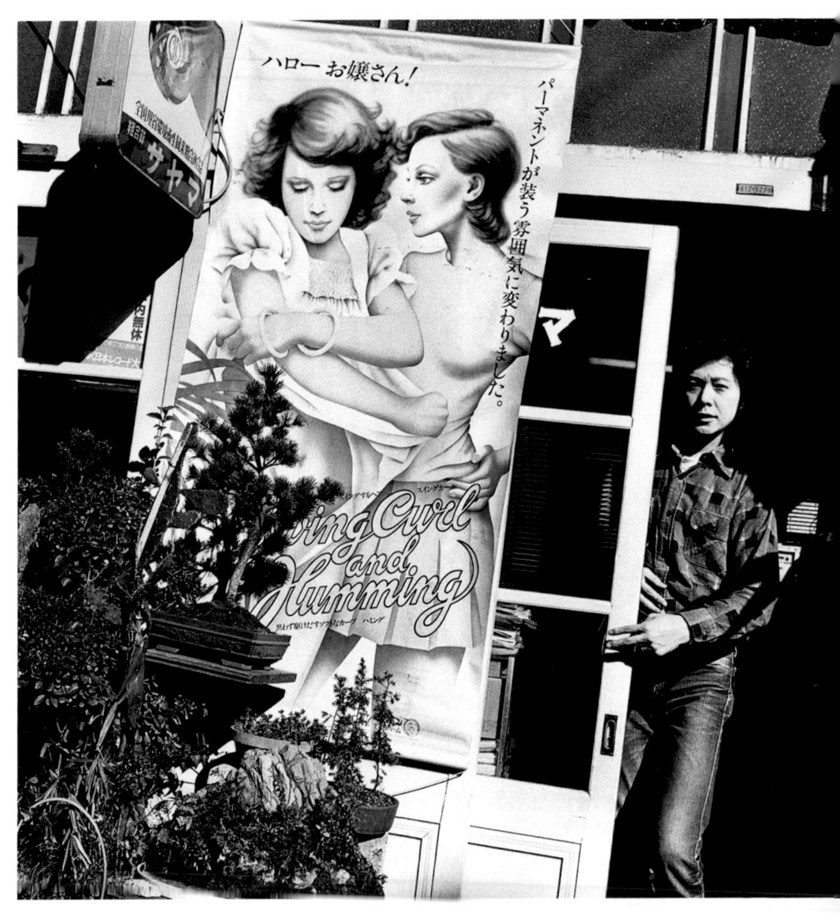

49. *Anonymous Man and Woman*, 1977.
50. *My Tokyo 100*, 1977.

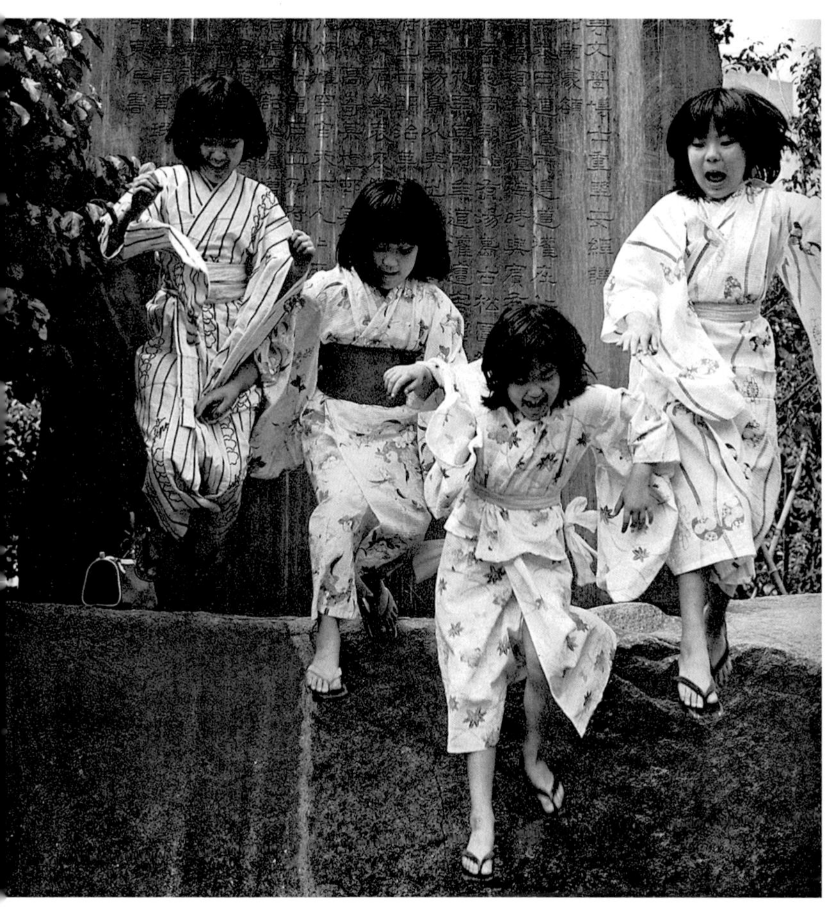

51. *Anonymous Man and Woman*, 1977.

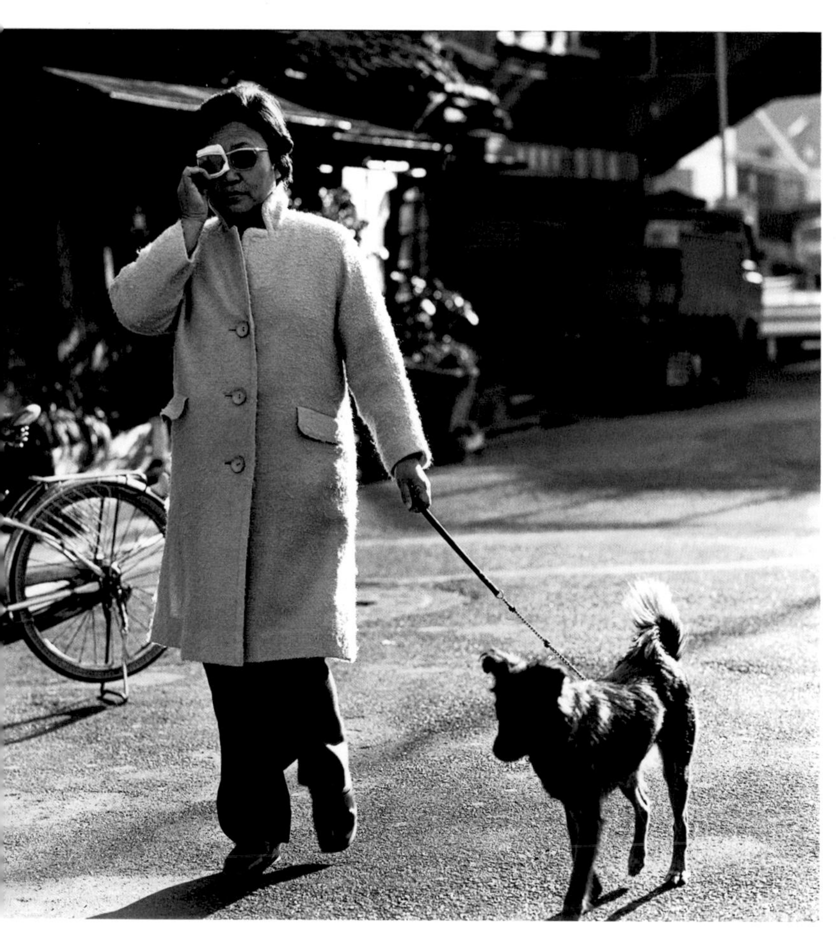

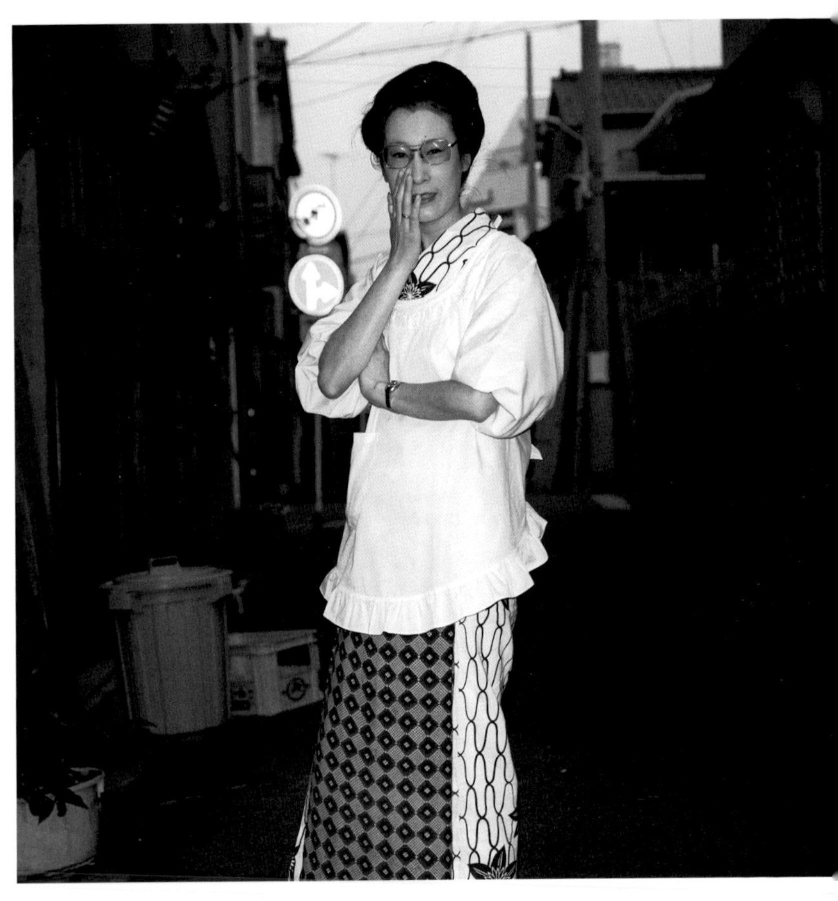

52. *My Tokyo 100*, 1978.

53. *Anonymous Man and Woman*, 1977.

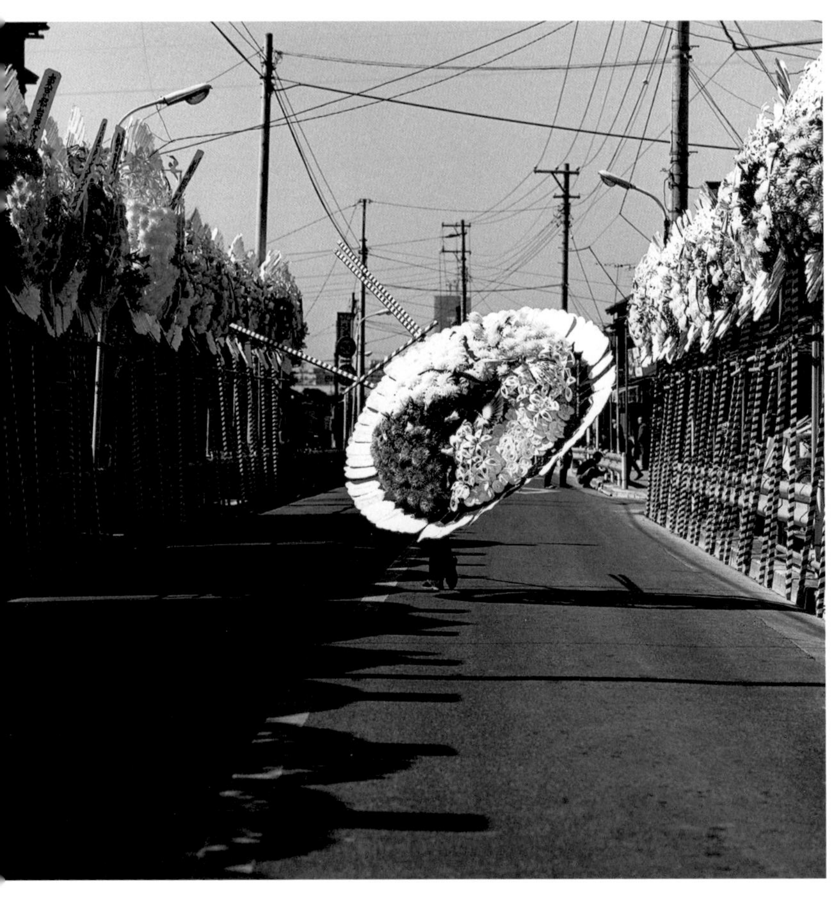

54. *Anonymous Man and Woman*, 1977.

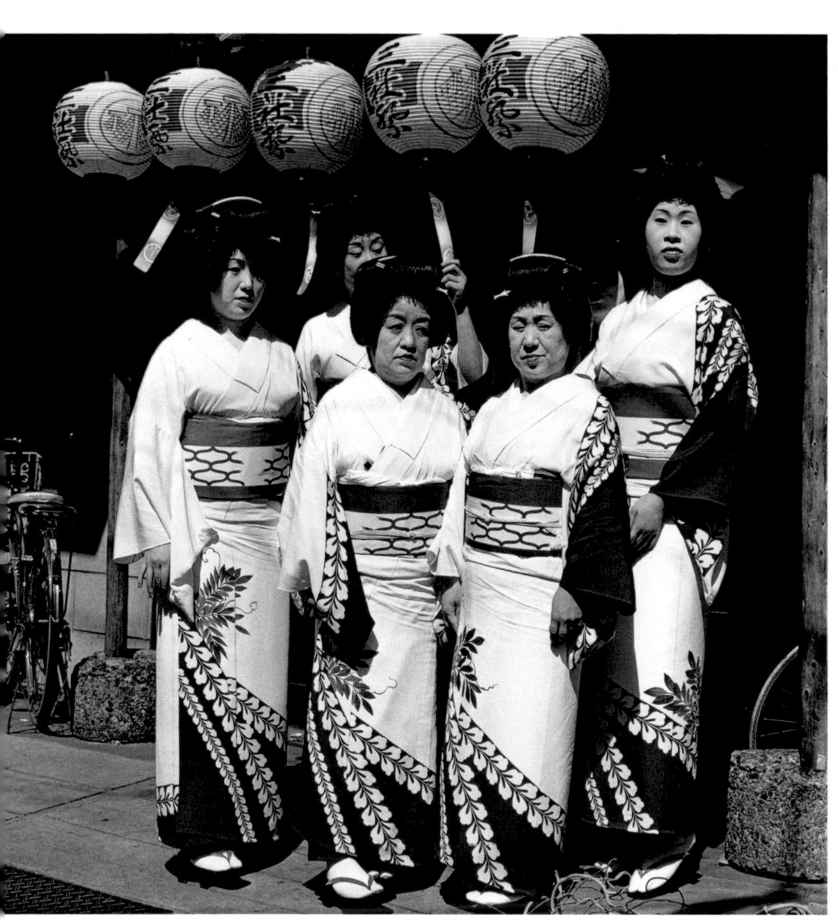

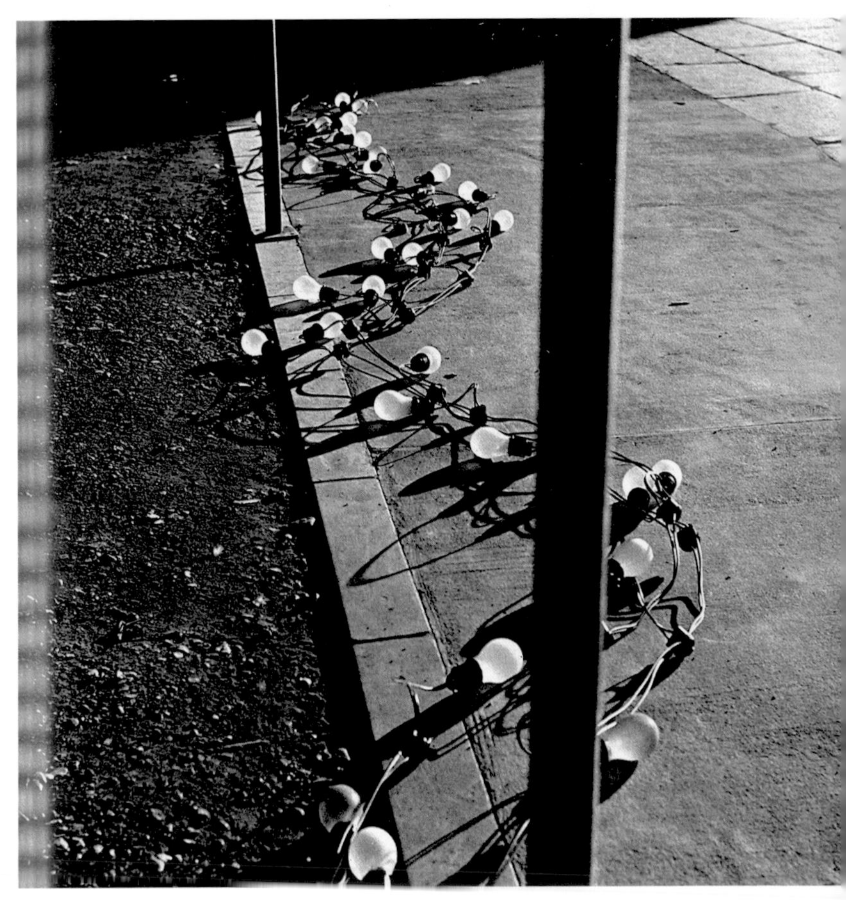

55. *My Tokyo 100*, 1976.
56. *Anonymous Man and Woman*, 1978.

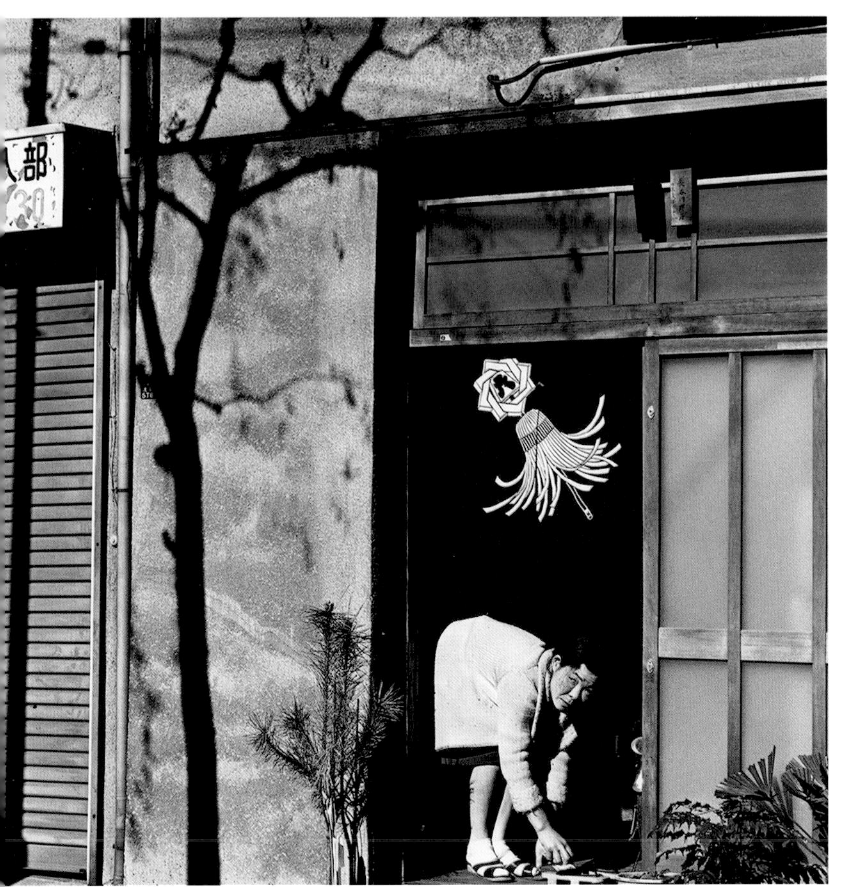

57. *My Tokyo 100*, 1977.

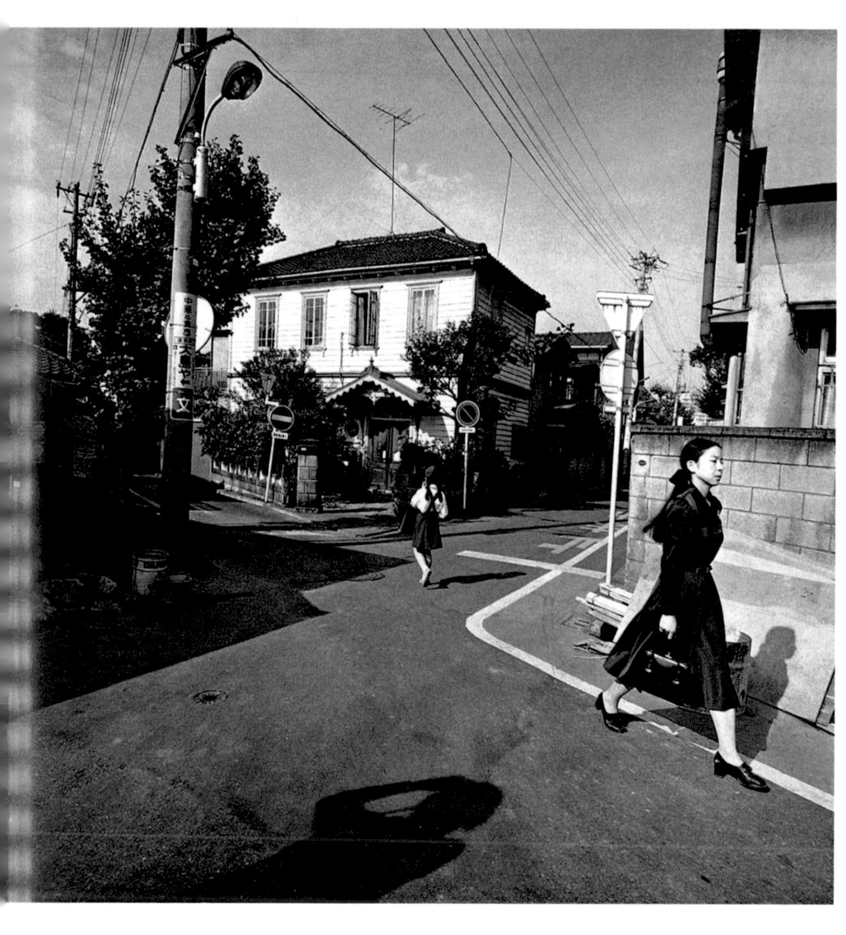

58. *My Tokyo 100*, 1977.

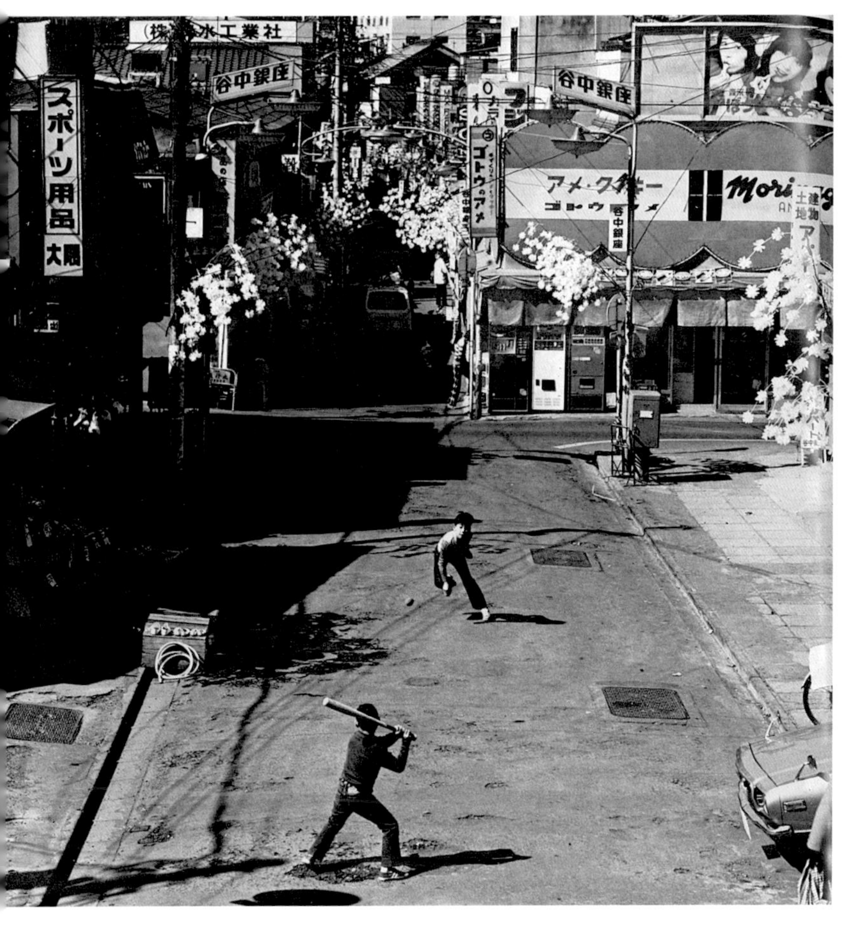

59. *My Tokyo 100*, 1977.

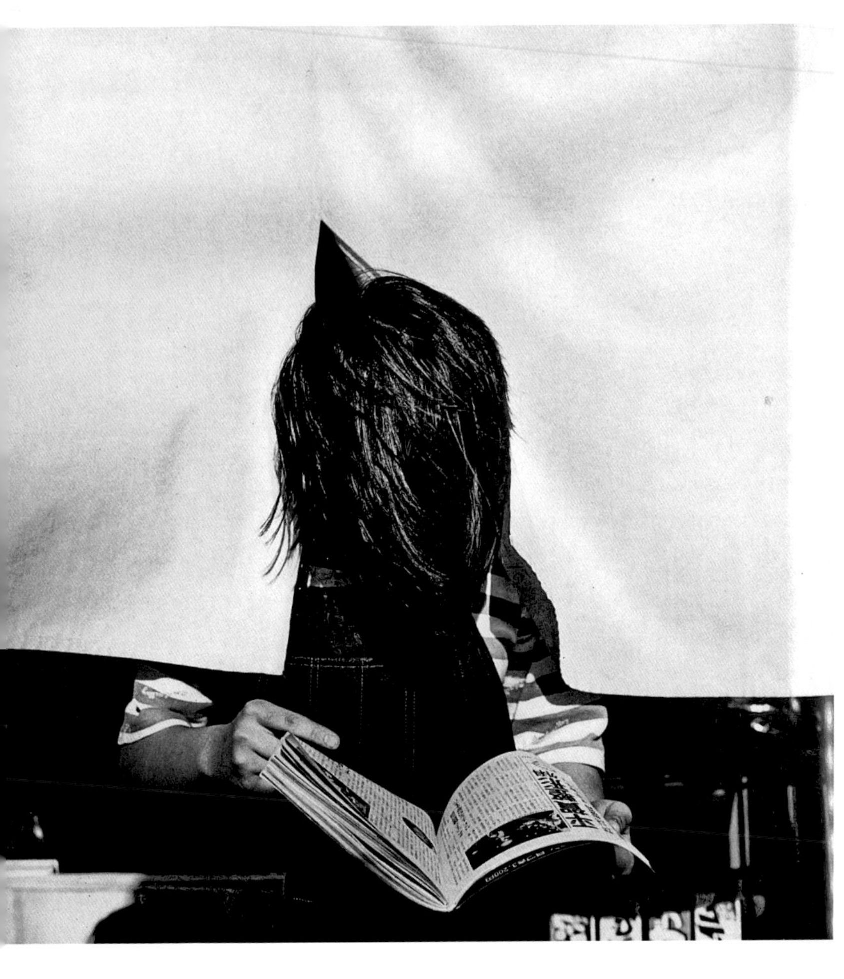

60. *My Tokyo 100*, 1977.

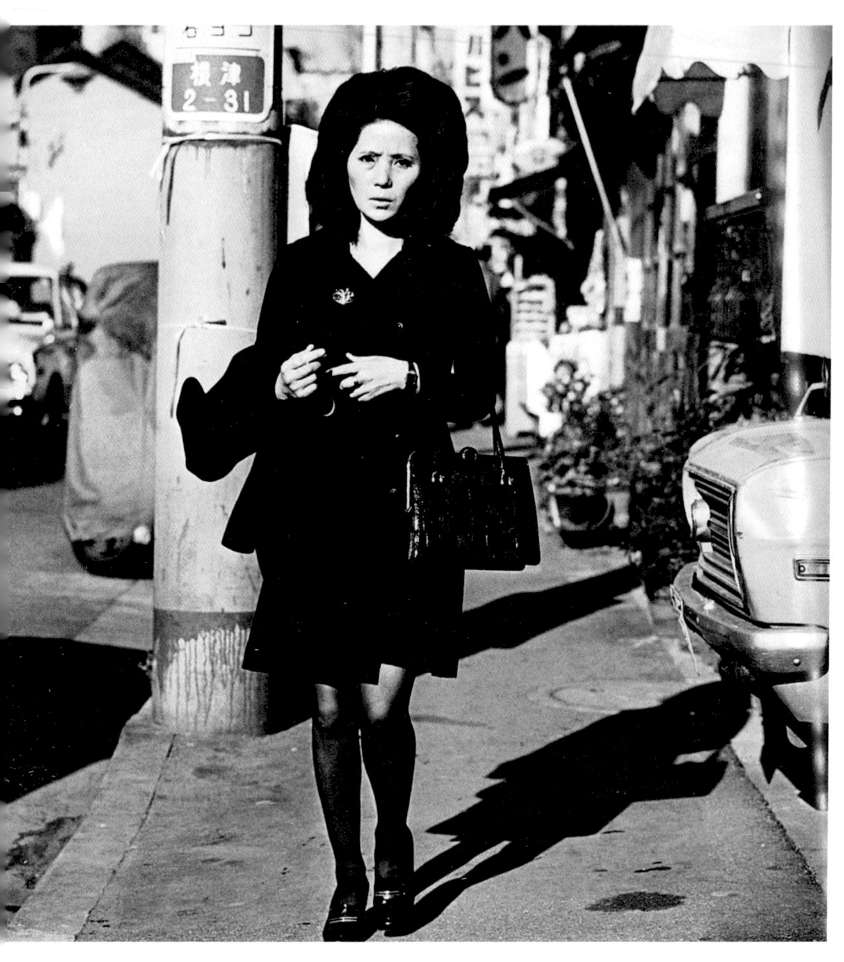

61. *Landscapes with Chimneys*, 1981.

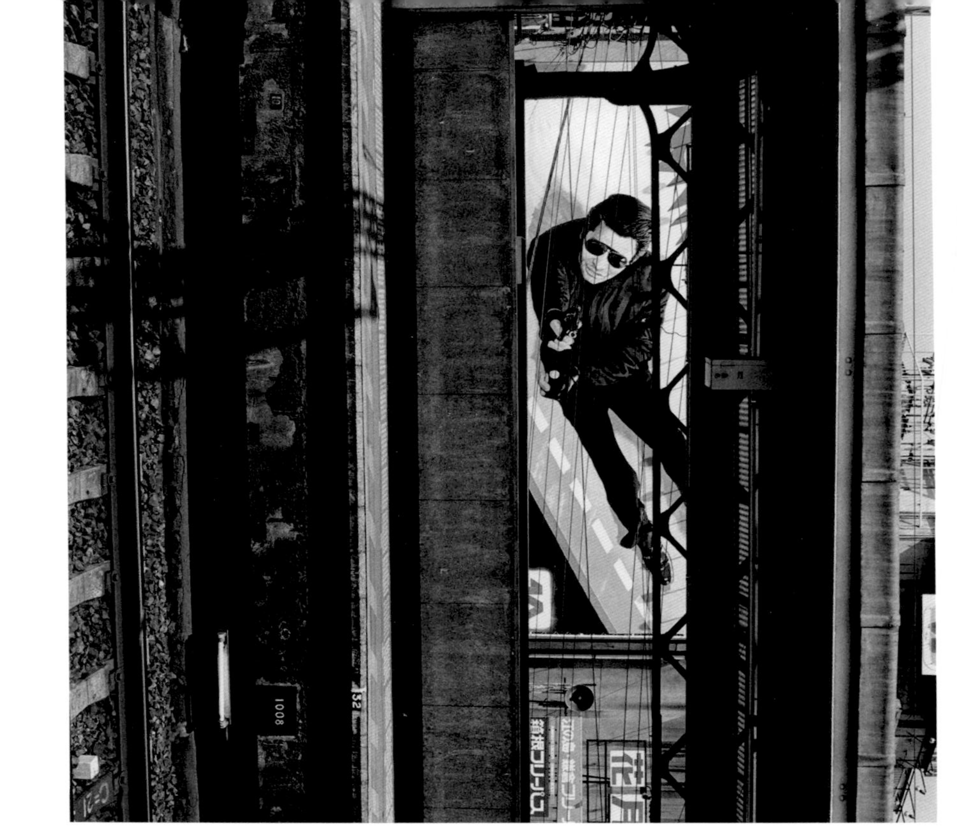
花月
箱根フリーパス

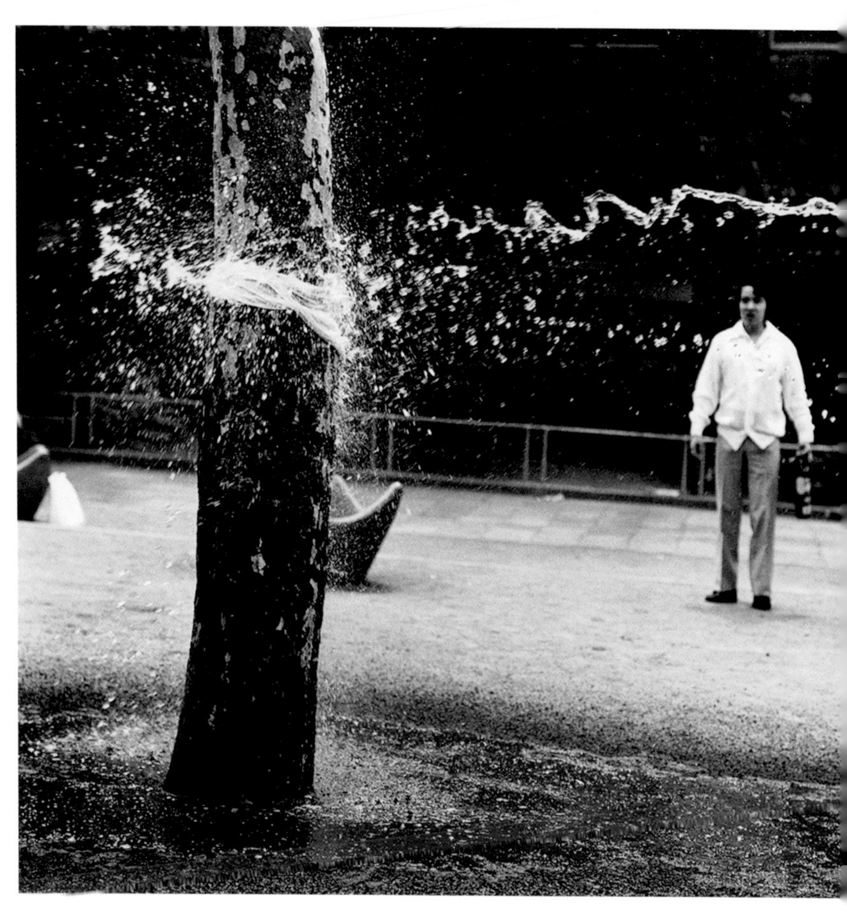

62. *Anonymous Man and Woman*, 1977.
63. *My Tokyo 100*, 1977.

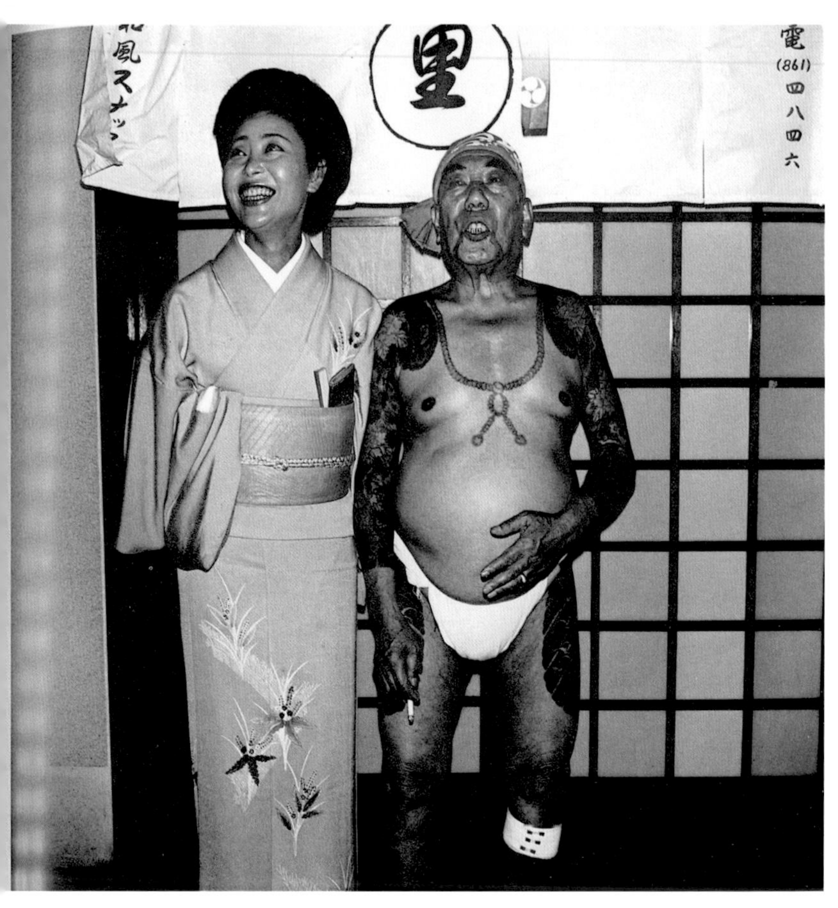

64. *My Tokyo 100*, 1977.

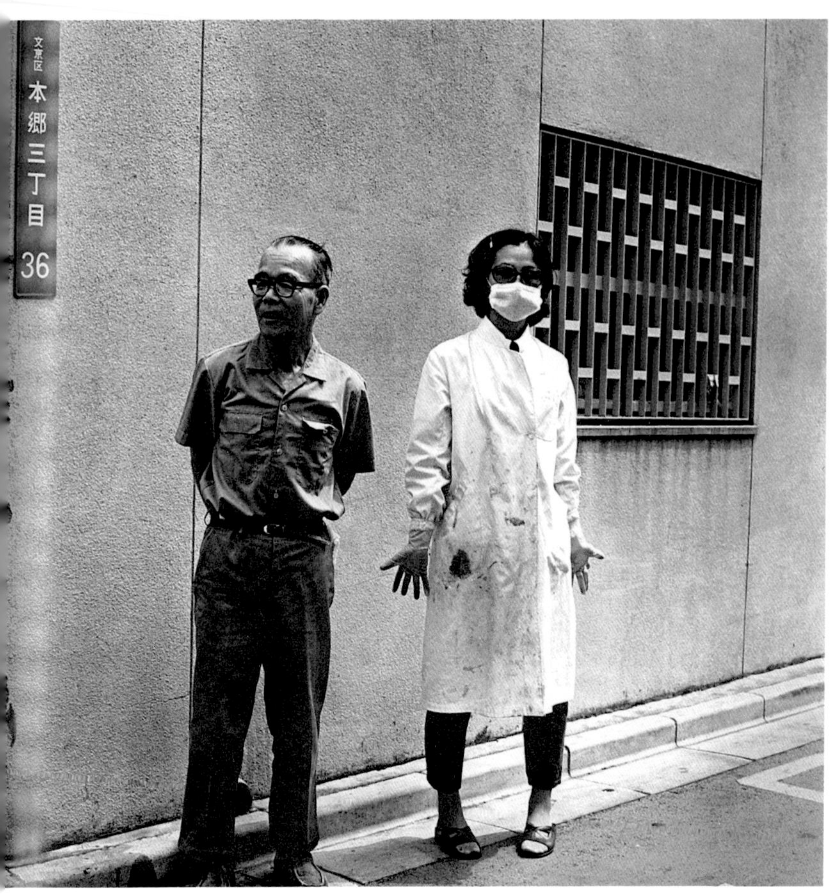
文京区
本郷三丁目
36

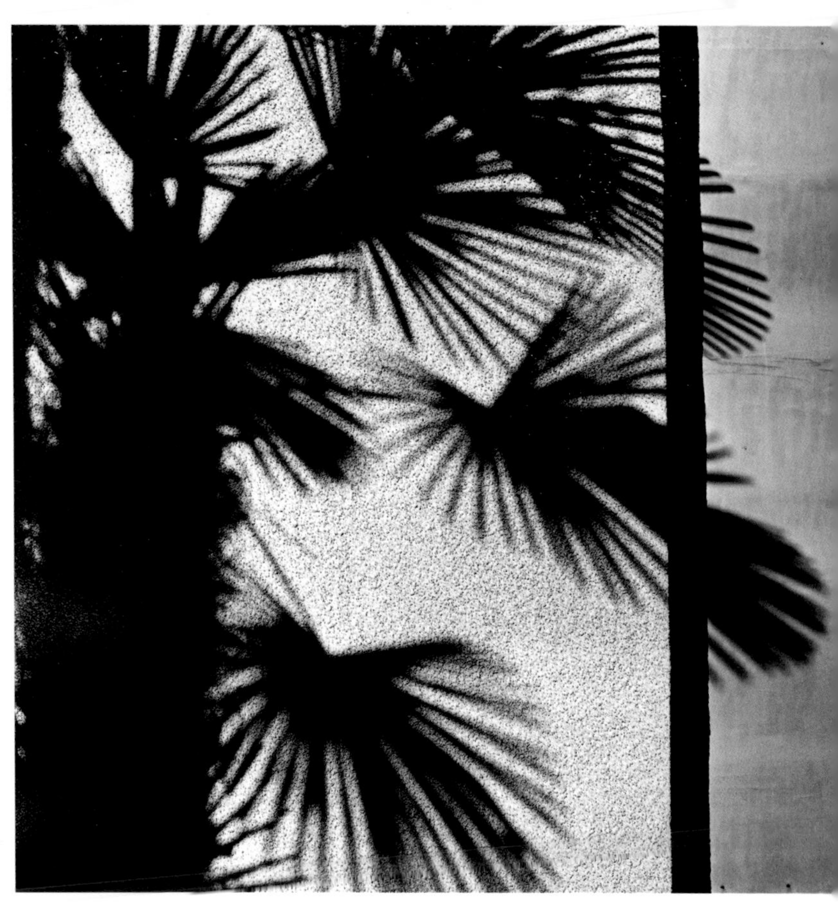

65. *A Solitary Camera At Large*, early 1970s.
66. *Anonymous Man and Woman*, 1977.

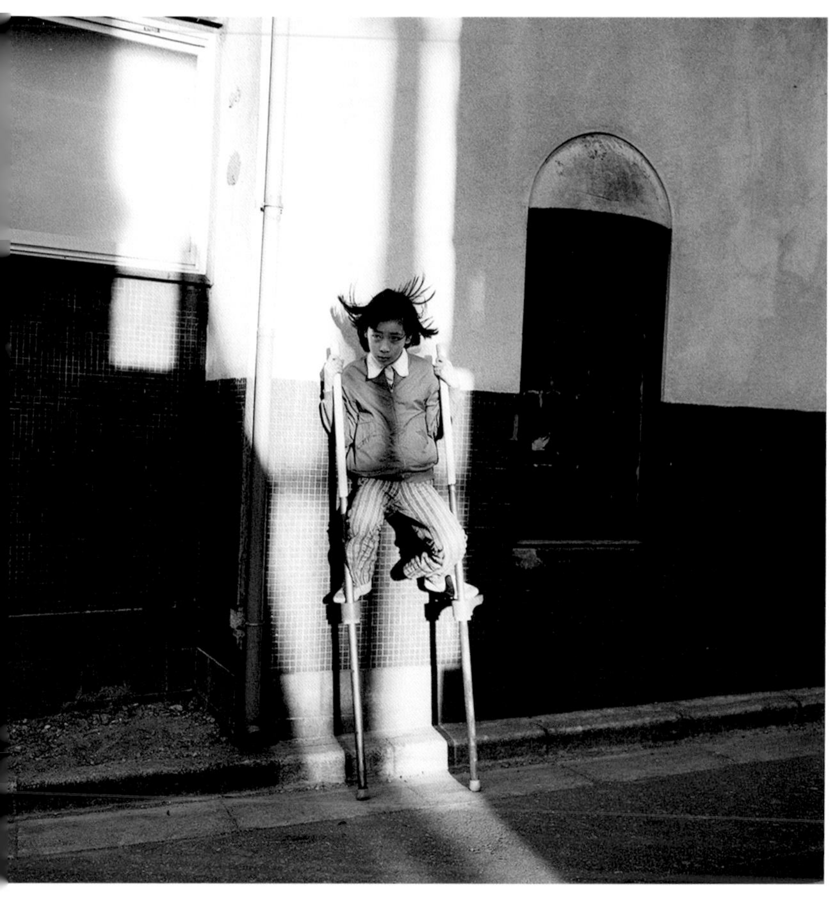

67. *78*, 1974.

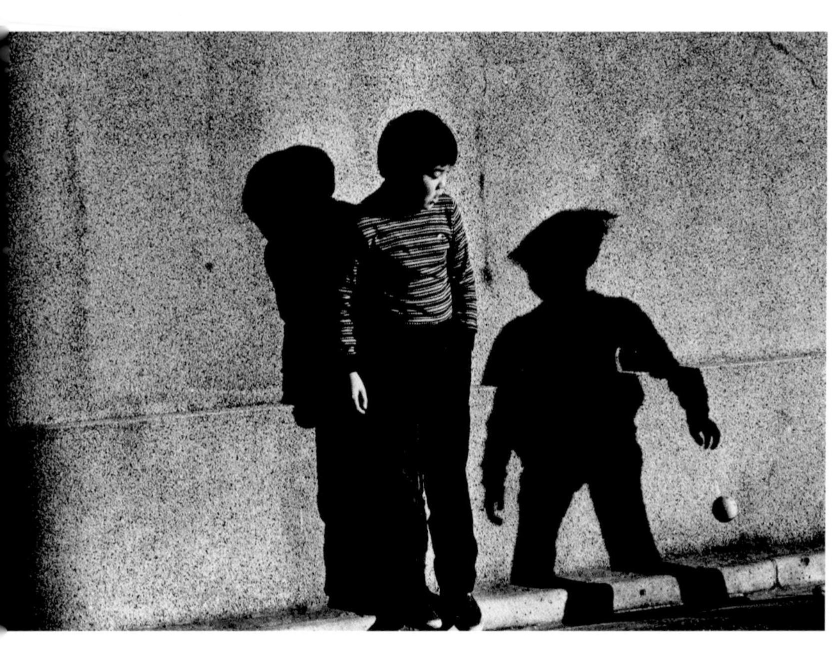

68. *Monogusa Shui*, 1982.

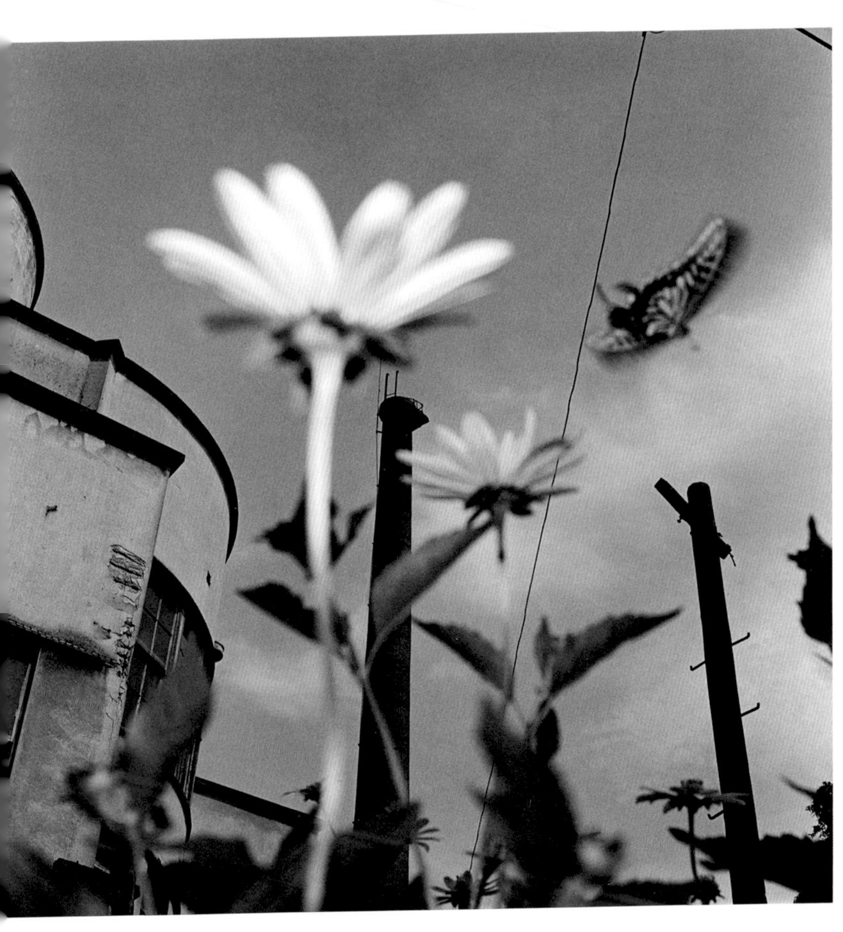

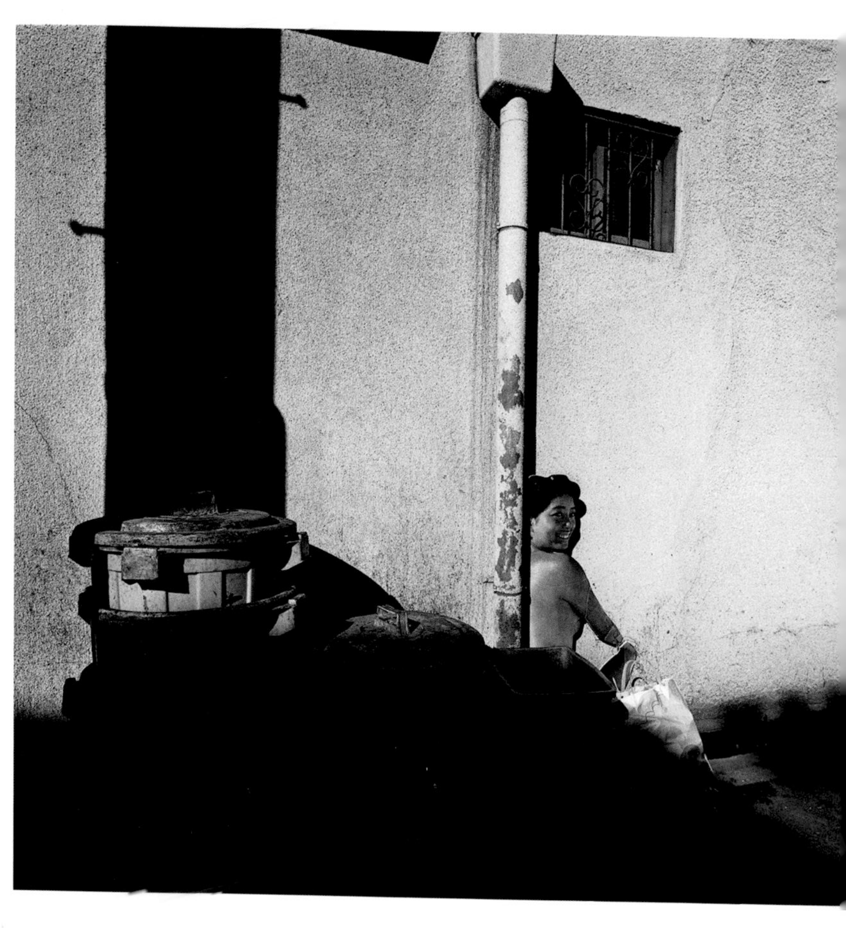

69. *Anonymous Man and Woman*, 1978.
70. *Monogusa Shui*, 1981.

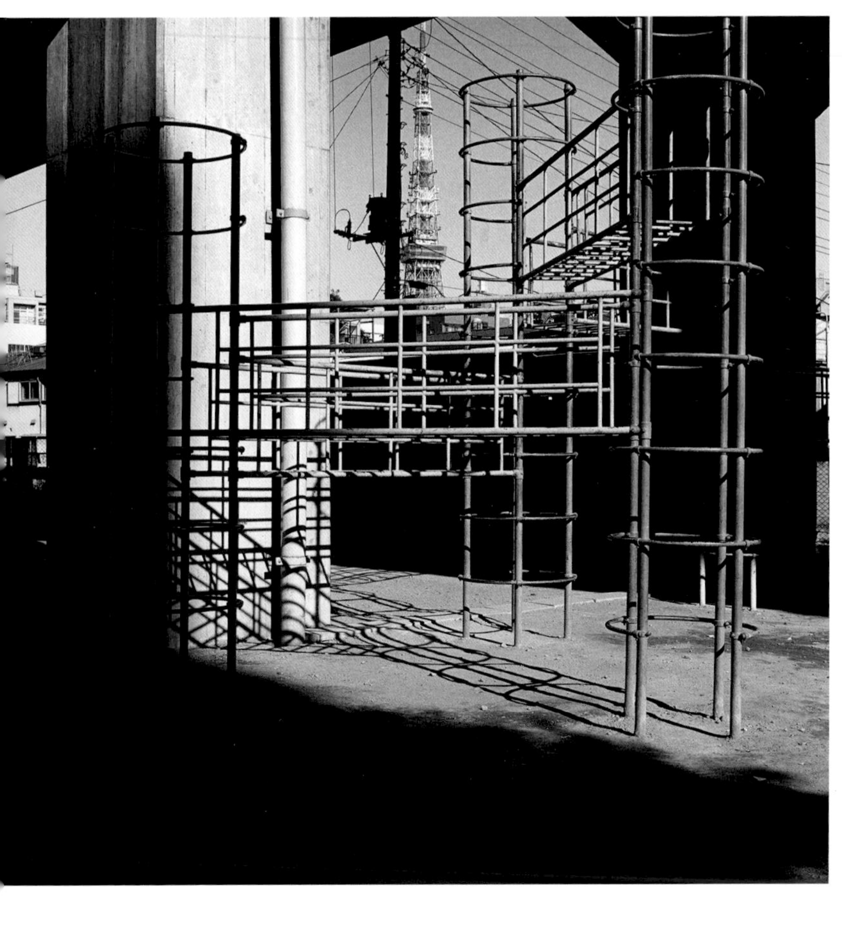

71. *Monogusa Shui*, 1981.

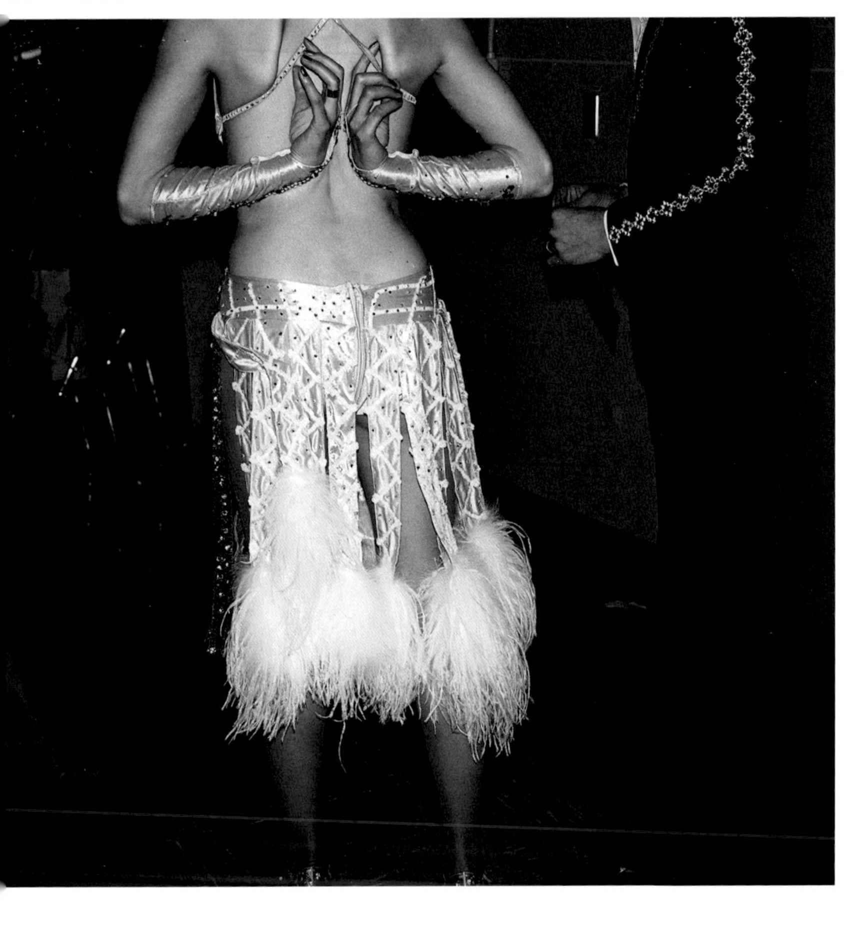

72. *The Sketch of Kanto Area*, 1982.

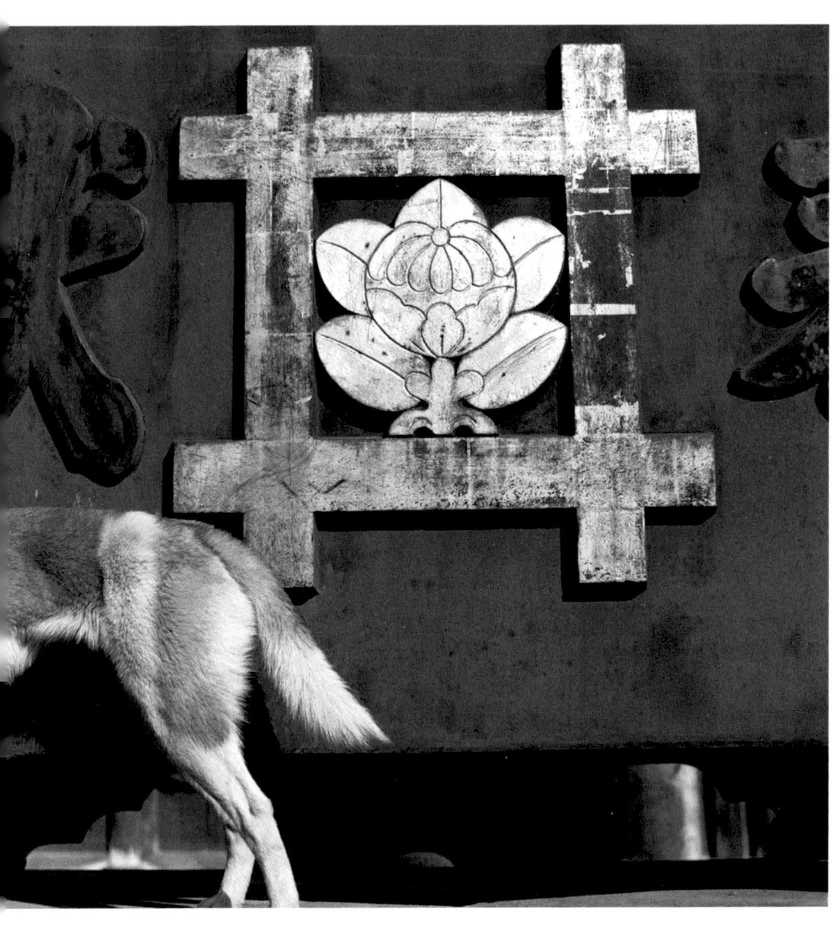

73. *The Sketch of Kanto Area*, 1982.

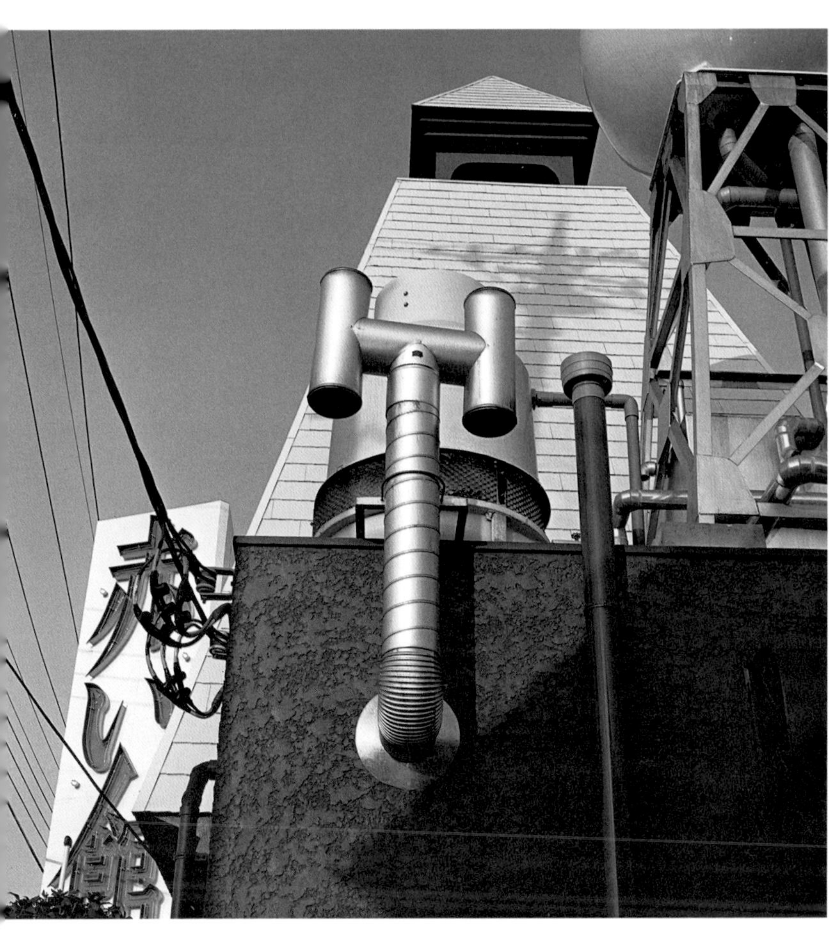

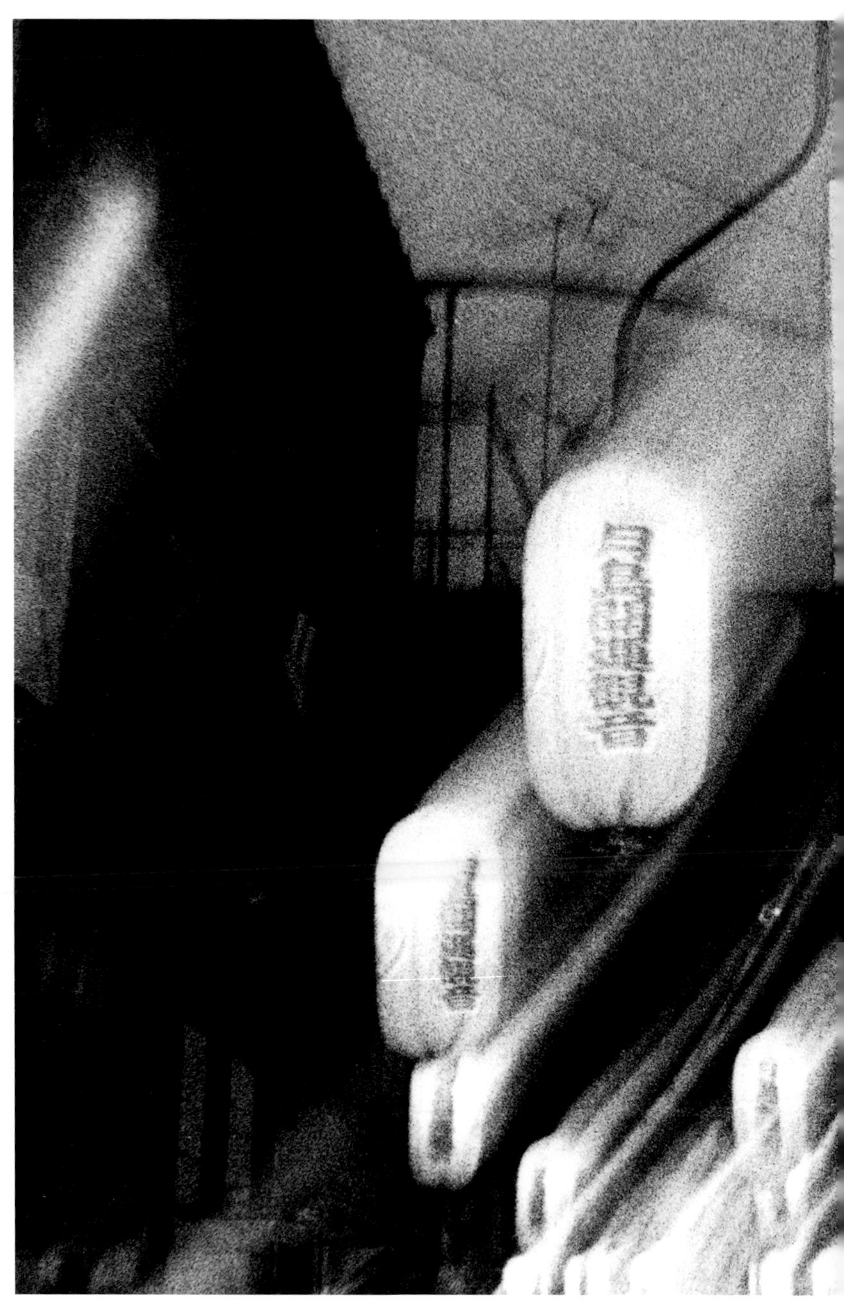

74. *Gankotoshi*, 1991.

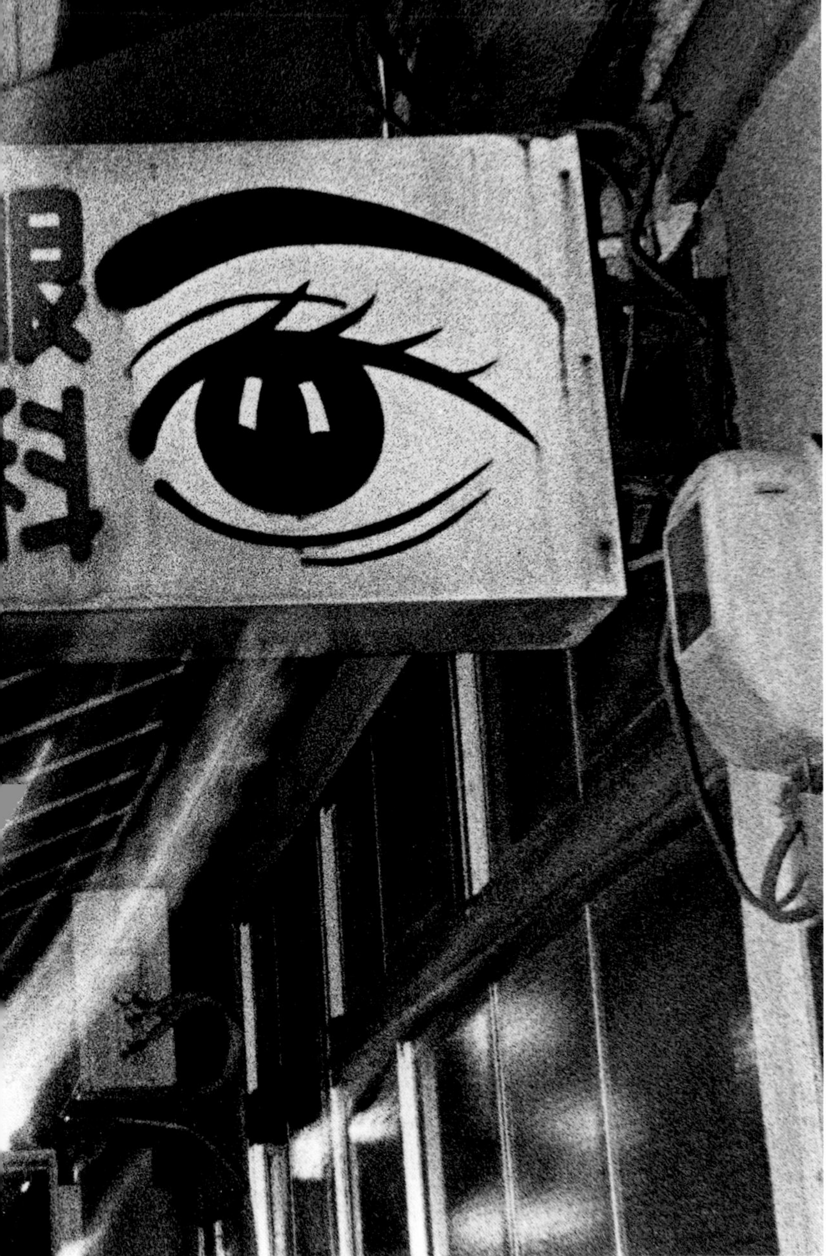

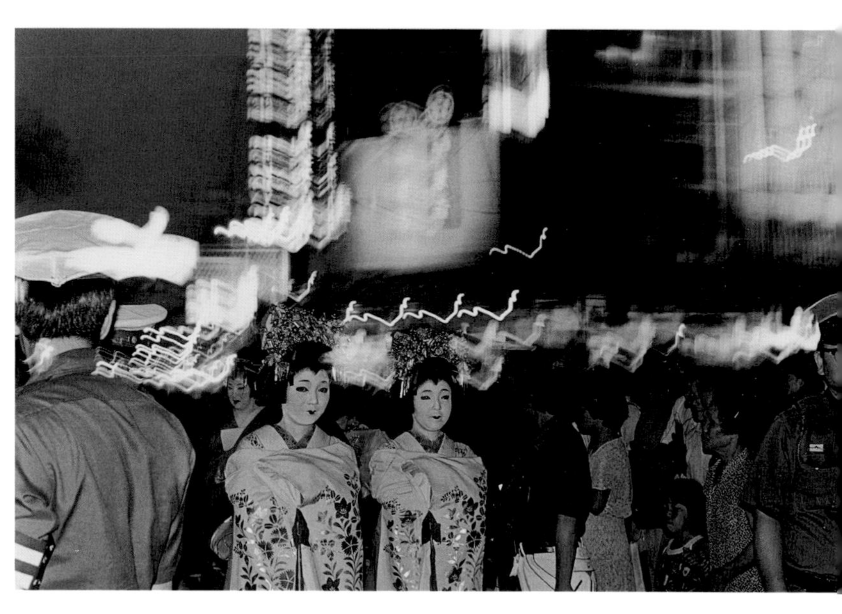

75. *Journey to the Tobacco Shop on the Corner*, 1979.
76. *Journey to the Tobacco Shop on the Corner*, 1980.

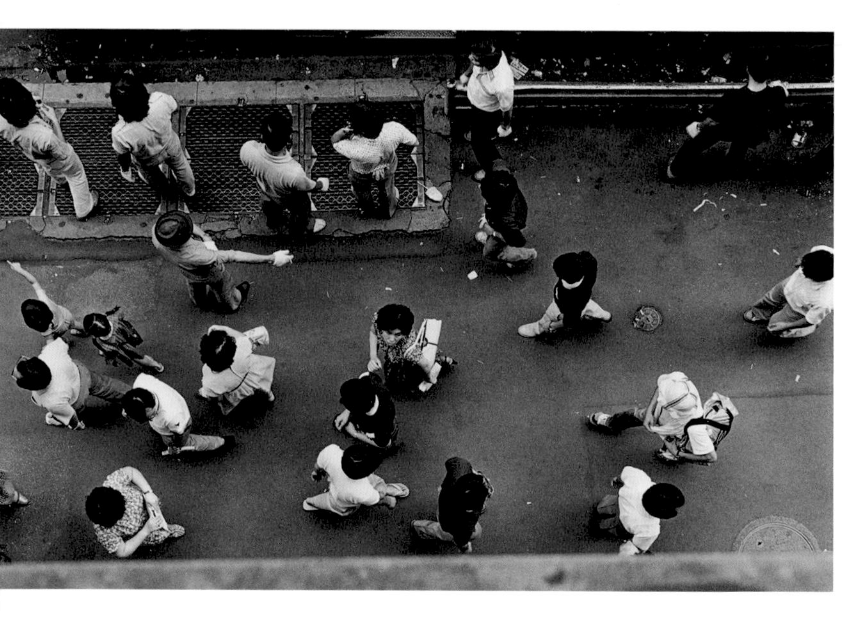

77. *Gankotoshi*, 1978.

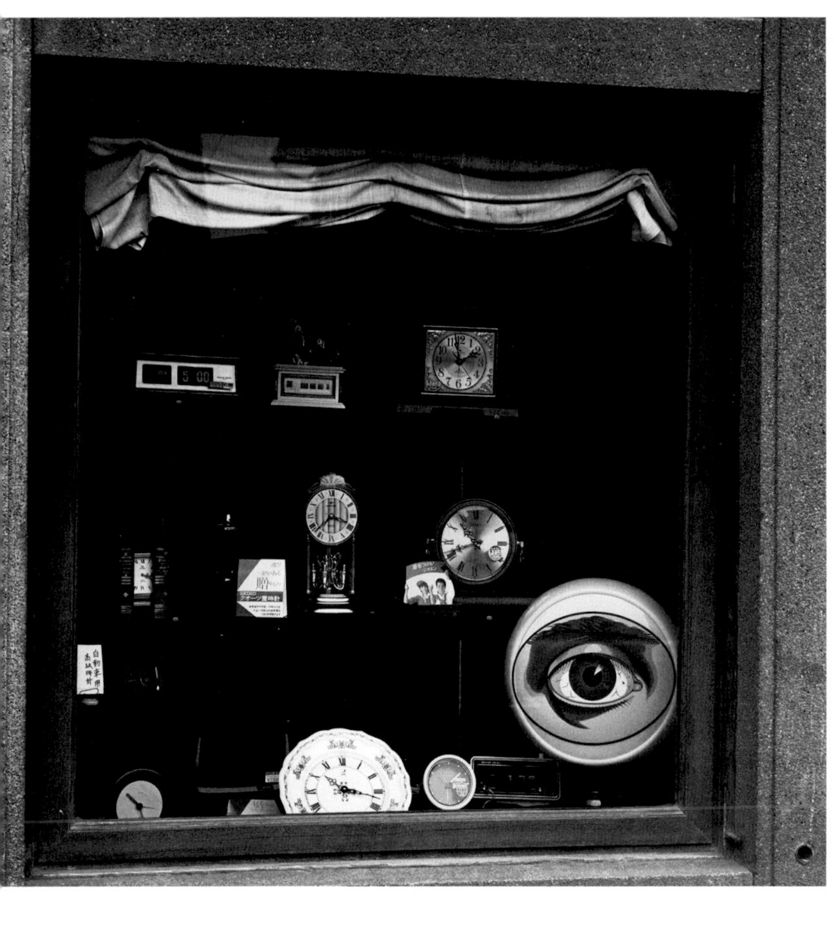

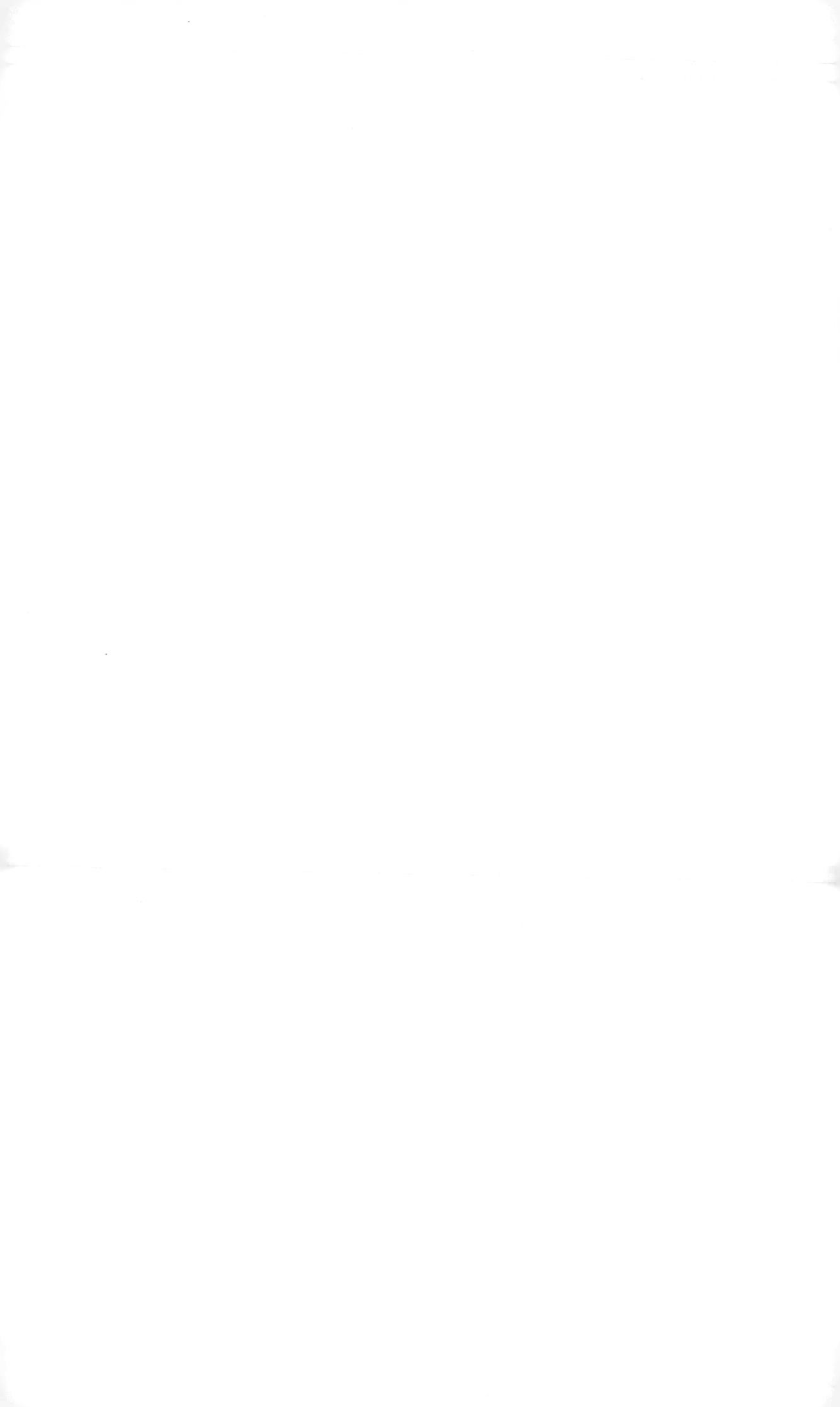

Biography

by Yuko Ikegami

1940 Kazumasa Suda is born on 24 April in Kanda, Tokyo. He is an only child. His father owns a bar.

1945 Suda's family seeks refuge in Urawa (Saitama prefecture) during the war. When they return to Kanda, his father runs a company that sells slates for roofs and chimneys. The boy who will become Issei Suda grows up in a well-off family during Japan's postwar economic boom. He roams the districts of Kanda and Jimbocho and becomes passionately interested in photography and film as a teenager.

1959 While studying law at Tōyō University, he frequents a local photographic studio run by Shigejiro Mori, where he absorbs photography books and magazines. He is invited to join Sonne Gruppe, a group that brings together professional (Haruo Itokawa and Eihan Nakano, among others) and amateur photographers, formed by first-year students at Tokyo College of Photography. Its members take a relaxed approach, finding subjects in everyday life or while travelling.

1961 Issei Suda drops out of university and joins Tokyo College of Photography, becoming a fourth-year student.

1962 After graduating from Tokyo College of Photography, he works for his father's company and devotes his free time to exploring new photographic techniques. Many of his fellow students achieve success over the years that follow, including Shinzō Hanabusa, Shisei Kuwabara, Kishin Shinoyama, Kazumi Kurigami and Taiji Arita.

1963 He is awarded a prize for best photographer of the year by the magazine *Nippon Camera* for his series *Osorezan e*.

1964 First in a long series of contributions to magazines including *Camera Jidai*, *Nippon Camera*, *Asahi Camera* and *Camera Mainichi*.

1967–70 He works as a still photographer for the avant-garde theatre troupe Tenjo Sajiki, founded by Shuji Terayama. He shares the latter's fascination with myth and folklore. He decides to leave his father's business and make a living as a professional photographer.

1969 First marriage.

1971 Becomes a freelance photographer and sets up his own studio.

1976 Wins the Newcomer's Award from the Photographic Society of Japan for his series *Fūshi Kaden*.

1975–77 Several images from his series *Fūshi Kaden* are published in the magazine *Camera Mainichi*, bringing him worldwide attention.

1978 His first monograph, *Fūshi Kaden*, is published by Asahi Sonorama.

1979–2003 Teaches at Tokyo College of Photography.

1985 Divorce and second marriage. Wins the Domestic Photographer Award at the Higashikawa Awards for his series *Fragment of Everyday Life*.

1986 Birth of his daughter.

1989–98 Teaches at Tokyo Zokei University.

1991–97 Opens the Hiranagacho-Bashi Gallery in Tokyo, which is run by his wife Yoshiko. He exhibits a lot of work by young artists there.

1997 Wins the Domon Ken Award for the book *Human Memory*, published in 1996.

2000–11 Teaches at Osaka University of Arts.

2001–13 Holds a series of photography workshops called Suda Issei Juku and devotes himself to promoting the training of young photographers.

2014 Given the Lifetime Achievement Award by the Photographic Society of Japan.

2019 Wins the 31st Society of Photography Awards Special Prize for his book *Fragment of Everyday Life* (2018). He dies in Chiba on 7 March, at the age of 78.

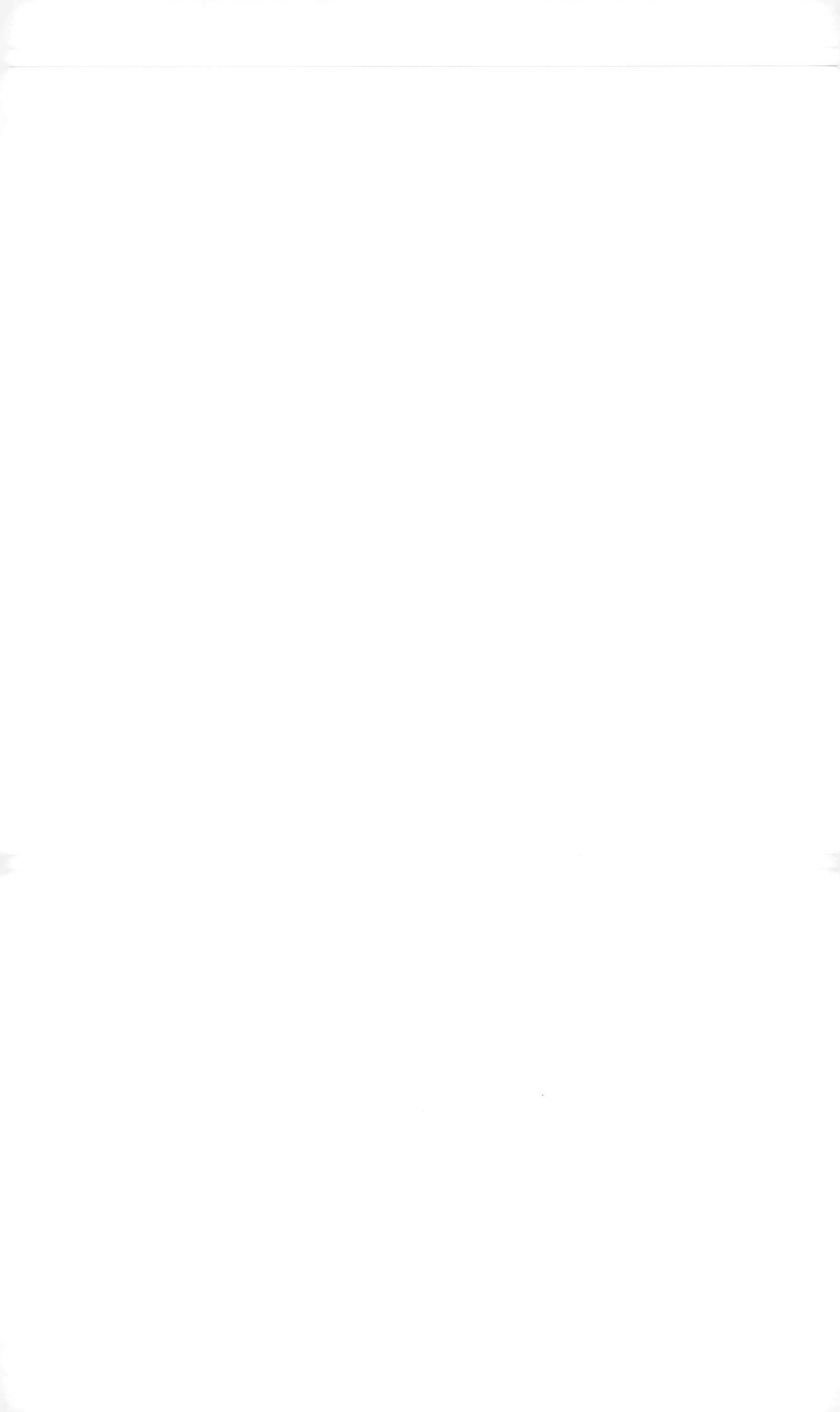

Selected bibliography

Fūshi Kaden, Tokyo: Asahi Sonorama, 1978;
new ed. Tokyo: Akio Nagasawa Publishing,
2012

My Tokyo 100, Tokyo: Nikkor Club, 1979;
new ed. Tokyo: Zen Foto Gallery, 2013

Dog's Nose, Tokyo: IPC, 1991

Trance Trunk, Tokyo: Shorin-sha, 1994

Human Memory, Tokyo: Creo, 1996

Suda Issei, Japanese Photographers, no. 40,
Tokyo: Iwanami Shoten, 1998

Akai Hana: Scarlet Bloom, Tokyo: Wides
Shuppan, 2000

Minyou Sanga, Tokyo: Tosei-sha, 2007

Journey to the Tobacco Shop on the Corner,
Tokyo: Place M, 2011

*Issei Suda: The Work of a Lifetime: Photographs
1968–2006*, Berlin: Only Photography, 2011

Six by Six, Set 4: Sparrow Island, Portland, OR:
Nazraeli Press, 2012

Rubber, Tokyo: Place M, 2012

1975 Miuramisaki, Tokyo: Akio Nagasawa
Publishing, 2012

Monogatari of Pines, Taipei: Aurastudio, 2013

Nagi no hira: Fragments of Calm, Tokyo:
Tosei-sha, 2013

Early Works 1970–1975, Tokyo: Akio Nagasawa
Publishing, 2013

Anonymous Man and Woman: Tokyo 1976–78,
Tokyo: Akio Nagasawa Publishing, 2013;
new ed. 2021

Tokyo-kei, Portland, OR: Nazraeli Press;
Tokyo: Zen Foto Gallery, 2013

Osorezan e / The Journey to Osorezan, Tokyo:
Zen Foto Gallery, 2013.

Kamagasaki Magic Lantern 2000–2014,
Tokyo: Zen Foto Gallery, 2015

Childhood Days, Tokyo: Akio Nagasawa
Publishing, 2015

Rei, Tokyo: Akio Nagasawa Publishing, 2015

Boso Fudoki, Tokyo: Super Labo, 2015

Suddenly, Tokyo: Place M, 2016

Sein, Tokyo: Super Labo, 2017

Kan-nagara, Tokyo: Place M, 2017

Fragment of Everyday Life, Kyoto: Seigensha
Art Publishing, Inc., 2018

The Mechanical Retina on My Fingertips,
Tokyo: Zen Foto Gallery, 2018

Landscapes with Chimneys, Tokyo: Place M,
2019

Gankotoshi, Tokyo: Akio Nagasawa Publishing,
2019

Tokyo Modern Pictorial, Tokyo: Zen Foto
Gallery, 2020

78, Marseille: Chose Commune, 2020

New Life, Tokyo: Akio Nagasawa Publishing,
2020

Eden, Tokyo: Place M, 2020

Family Diary, Marseille: Chose Commune, 2021

The Sketch of Kanto Area, Tokyo: Akio
Nagasawa Publishing, 2022

Holy Night, Marseille: Chose Commune, 2022

Selected exhibitions

Solo shows

1977 *Fūshi Kaden*, Ginza-Shinjuku Nikon Salon, Tokyo; Osaka Nikon Salon, Osaka.

1978 *Issei Suda*, Camp, Tokyo.
Anonymous Man and Woman: Tokyo 1976–78, Ginza-Shinjuku Nikon Salon, Tokyo.
Fūshi Kaden, Canon Photo Gallery, Amsterdam.

1979 *Misuzukaru shinano*, Minolta Photo Space, Tokyo/ Osaka.
Issei Suda: Original Print Exhibition, Tsukaido, Fukuoka.

1981 *My Tokyo*, Sicof, Milan.

1982 *Monogusa Shui*, Annual Award from the Photographic Society of Japan, Nagase Photo Salon, Tokyo.

1983 *Issei Suda Show*, Shadai Gallery, Tokyo Polytechnic University.

1985 *Fragment of Everyday Life*, Olympus Gallery, Tokyo.

1986 *Tsugaru enkin*, Polaroid Gallery, Tokyo.

1987 *The Big Picture*, International Month of Photography, Athens.

1988 *Taipei White Heat*, Doi Photo Plaza Shibuya, Tokyo.

1989 *Issei Suda Photo Exhibition*, Niihama Municipal Native Art Museum, Ehime.

1991 *Dog's Nose*, Minolta Photo Space, Tokyo.

1992 *Taipei gaishi*, Kaohsiung Public Library, Taiwan.

1993 *Naked City*, Doi Photo Plaza Shibuya, Tokyo.

1994 *Trance*, Zeit-Foto Salon, Tokyo.

1995 *Landscape of Japan 1988–1993*, Fuji Photo Salon, Tokyo.

1996 *Eclipse*, Konica Plaza, Tokyo.

1997 *Human Memory*, Ken Domon Museum of Photography, Yamagata.

1998 *Hello Vietnam*, Ginza Nikon Salon, Tokyo.

1999 *Fūshi Kaden*, Internationale Fototage Herten, Germany.
Sequence, Tokyo Photographic Culture Centre.

2000 *Issei Suda*, Osaka University of Arts.

2001 *Rubber*, Gallery Past Rays, Kanagawa.

2002 *Typhoon-Okinawa*, Tokyo Photographic Culture Centre.
Eden, Gallery Past Rays, Kanagawa.

2003 *Vietnam*, Osaka University of Arts.
Figure, Gallery Past Rays, Kanagawa.

2004 *Osaka*, Nadar, Osaka.

2005 *Eden: the Last Chapter*, Nadar, Osaka.

2006 *Kineticscape*, Gallery Past Rays, Tokyo.

2007 *My Tokyo from Yokohama Museum of Art Collection*, Yokohama Museum of Art, Kanagawa.

2008 *1987 Taipei gaishi*, Gallery Past Rays, Kanagawa.

2009 *4-Chome, Ginza, Tokyo 2008–2009*, Place M, Tokyo.

2010 *Vintage Photographs 1970s and 80s*, Higher Pictures, New York.

2011 *Sparrow Island*, Photo Gallery International, Tokyo.

2012 *Fūshi Kaden*, BLD Gallery, Tokyo.

2013 *Issei Suda: Photographs*, Charles A. Hartman Fine Art, Portland, OR.
Nagi no hira: Fragments of Calm, Tokyo Metropolitan Museum of Photography.

2014 *Waga Tokyo*, Zen Foto Gallery, Tokyo.
Issei Suda: Life in Flower: 1971–1977, Miyako Yoshinaga Gallery, New York.

2015 *Rei*, Akio Nagasawa Gallery, Tokyo.
Childhood Days, Aura Gallery, Beijing.

2017 *Fūshi Kaden: Momat Collection*, National Museum of Modern Art, Tokyo.

2018 *Childhood Days*, Akio Nagasawa Gallery, Tokyo.

2019 *Gankotoshi*, Akio Nagasawa Gallery, Tokyo.

2020 *Eden*, Place M, Tokyo.

2021 *My Japan*, FOMU, Antwerp.

Group shows

1976 *Neue Fotografie aus Japan*, Stadtmuseum, Graz.

1978 Photokina, Kolnischer Kunstverein, Cologne.

1979 *Japanese Photography Today and Its

Origin, Galleria d'Arte Moderna, Bologna; Palazzo Reale, Milan; Palais des Beaux-Arts, Brussels; Institute of Contemporary Arts, London.
Five Men Show, Santa Fe Gallery of Photography, Santa Fe, NM.
Japan: A Self-Portrait, International Center of Photography, New York.
1981 *Robert Mapplethorpe, Issei Suda*, Forum Stadtpark, Graz.
1983 *Issei Suda & Diane Arbus*, Zeit-Foto Salon, Tokyo.
A Scene of Contemporary Japanese Art 2: An Encounter With the Sights Around Us, Miyagi Museum of Art.
1985 *Paris/New York/Tokyo*, Tsukuba Museum of Photography, Ibaraki.
1986 *Fotografi a Japonesa Contemporánea*, Casa Elizalde, Barcelona.
1987 *The International Month of Photography*, Hellenic Centre for Photography, Athens.
Empathy: Contemporary Japanese Photography, Visual Studies Workshop, Rochester.
1988 *Eight Japanese Photographers*, Photo Gallery International, Tokyo.
1989 *Eleven Photographers in Japan 1965–1975*, Yamaguchi Prefectural Art Museum.
The Hitachi Collection of Contemporary Japanese Photography, Center for Creative Photography, University of Arizona, Tucson, AZ.
150 Years of Photography, Konica Plaza, Tokyo.
Europalia 89 Japan, FOMU, Antwerp; Musée de la Photographie, Charleroi.
Photography 150 Years: Its Light and Shadow – Inventory of Photographs Collection, Printemps Ginza, Tokyo.
1990 *Foto Biënnale Rotterdam*, Perspektief, Rotterdam.
Tokyo: A City Perspective, Tokyo Metropolitan Museum of Photography.
1991 *Japanese Photography in the 1970s: Memories Frozen in Time*, Tokyo Metropolitan Museum of Photography.
1992 *What Were Photographers Expressing: 1960–1980*, Konica Plaza, Tokyo.

Photography & Climatology II, Miyagi Museum of Art.
1995 *Tokyo/City of Photos*, Tokyo Metropolitan Museum of Photography.
1996 *Japanese Photography – Form In/Out, Part 2: The Transformation of Photography in the Post-War Era, 1945–1980*, Tokyo Metropolitan Museum of Photography.
1998 Photokina, Messegelände, Rheinhallen, Cologne.
1999 *Vintage Prints Represent the Zeitgeist*, Zeit-Foto Salon, Tokyo.
2000 *23 Japanese Photographers*, Photo Gallery International, Tokyo.
2001 *Exploring Photography 2*, National Museum of Modern Art, Tokyo.
2002 *Human Image*, Kawasaki City Museum, Kanagawa.
Past Rays Collection, Gallery Past Rays, Kanagawa.
Letter, Sumiso, Osaka.
2003 *Japanese Photography: A Distinctive Aesthetic*, Museum of Fine Arts, Houston.
Japanese Photography 1970's–1980's, S. K. Josefsberg Studio, Portland, OR.
Oirase Information Terminal Photo Collection, Hanamizuki Hall, NHK Hachinohe, Aomori.
All Friends: The Photographers Who Met in 26 Years in Zeit-Foto Salon, Zeit-Foto Salon, Tokyo.
Mask of Japan, Aura Gallery, Shanghai.
2005 *Modern Masters of Photography: Japan*, Prudential Tower, Tokyo.
2006 *Memories of Showa*, Gunma Museum of Art, Tatebayashi.
2007 *Showa: Photography 1945–1989*, Tokyo Metropolitan Museum of Photography.
Exhibition from the Modern Japanese Photography: Collection of the Yamaguchi Prefectural Museum of Art, Tonami Art Museum, Ishikawa.
2008 *Self/Other*, The National Museum of Modern Art, Tokyo.
2009 *Strange Lands*, Tokyo Metropolitan Museum of Photography.
New Art 2009, Yokohama Civic Art Gallery, Kanagawa.
Showa: Photography 1945–1989,

Marugame Genichiro-Inokuma Museum
of Contemporary Art (MIMOCA), Kagawa.

2010 *The Here in There*, Salon de Verre,
Nagano.
Human Images of 20th Century, Tokyo
Metropolitan Museum of Photography.

2011 *Harmony of Nature and Humans*,
Gunma Museum of Art, Tatebayashi.
Photographs of Children, Tokyo Metropolitan
Museum of Photography.

2012 *Exhibition of Ken Domon Award: Winning
Works and Works of Ken Domon*, Ken Domon
Museum of Photography, Yamagata.
Japanese Photography in 1960's–1970's,
Dong Gang Museum of Photography,
Yeongwol, South Korea.
Tokyo 1955–1970: A New Avant-Garde,
Museum of Modern Art, New York.

2013 *Scandal: Nude*, BLD Gallery, Tokyo.

The Photofile series is the original English-language edition of the Photo Poche collection. It was first published between 1986 and 1992 by the Centre National de la Photographie, Paris, with the support of the French Ministry of Culture. Robert Delpire (1926–2017) was the creator of the series and its managing editor until 2017.

General editor: Géraldine Lay

Series design by Matthew Young

First published in the United Kingdom in 2024 by
Thames & Hudson Ltd, 181A High Holborn, London WC1V 7QX

First published in the United States of America in 2024 by
Thames & Hudson Inc., 500 Fifth Avenue, New York, New York 10110

Photo Poche © 2024 Actes Sud, France
Photographs © SUDA ISSEI Works
This edition © 2024 Thames & Hudson Ltd, London

British Library Cataloguing-in-Publication Data
A catalogue record for this book is available from the British Library

Library of Congress Control Number 2024935666

ISBN 978-0-500-29735-3

Printed and bound in Italy

Be the first to know about our new releases,
exclusive content and author events by visiting
thamesandhudson.com
thamesandhudsonusa.com
thamesandhudson.com.au